Unbroken Service:
A History of the
Mobile Police Department,
First Edition
2025

By
Captain
Billie Leonard Rowland

Book designed and formatted by Carrie Dalby Cox
Published by Jarvis V. Cushing Publishing
Mobile, Alabama

Title and chapter fonts in Libre Baskerville - italic

For Laury
and the Men and Women who have served
on the finest Police Department in the Country,
the Mobile Police Department

Table of Contents

Author's Note

The following pages are comprised of information gathered over several years. The information comes from the Mobile Police Department archives, City of Mobile Archives, the Mobile Public Library, the Historic Mobile Preservation Society Archives, the University of Alabama Special Collections Library, Mobile History Museum, old city directories, news articles, firsthand knowledge, and oral histories obtained by interviews.

Major Wilbur Williams (ret) conducted extensive research in the early 1990s and has been invaluable in making this possible. Gloria Reed at the Mobile County Personnel Board was always ready to help with research. Carrie Dalby Cox, a local author, was instrumental in the editing and publishing process for this book. Additionally, she spent numerous hours researching items for me and supplying countless books for my research, and I cannot thank her enough for her assistance. Elizabeth Theris-Boone, the manager of the Local History and Genealogy Division of the Mobile Public Library, was invaluable in obtaining information from the 1940s. I would also like to thank Charles "Chuck" Torrey from the Mobile History Museum, Bob Peck from the Historic Mobile Preservation Society Archives, Tilmon Brown, with Catholic Cemetery, William Smith and Alex Boucher, at the University of Alabama Special Collections Library. Sergeant Gerry Smith (retired) was gracious in allowing me to share some of his cartoons that I have collected. And I would like to thank Marilyn Johnston for her help with editing and formatting.

The City of Mobile Police Museum contained countless documents and parts of our history, including photographs that are included. The museum is now closed, but the items that it contained are securely stored until a new property can be secured to display them again. Some sections of this history will have gaps in dates and known information. Many documents and photographs have been lost, during departmental moves in 1950 and again in 1991. These are highlights that were found in different archives. Other information on specific individuals or events will be separated into their own sections.

Reproductions of letters or other documents are written as they are found in the original. Spelling or formatting mistakes or older terminology have not been corrected.

Introduction

The City of Mobile was founded in 1702. Between that founding and 1814, there is little known about the enforcement of laws in the city. The Territory of Alabama was created out of Mississippi Territory on August 15, 1817, and admitted to the United States on December 14, 1819, as the 22nd State.

In Mobile's history, she has been governed by six governments. First, by the French, from the founding of Mobile by Iberville and Bienville in 1702 to October 20, 1763, when the French ceded the territory to the English. The English ruled from October 20, 1763, to early 1780 when the territory was ceded to Spain. Spain took control of Mobile and the region in early 1780 and held it until May 14, 1812. On that date, the United States gained control of Mobile by treaty, and it became part of the Mississippi Territory that had been created in 1798. The city, though officially a part of the United States, was still guarded by the Spanish. She did not come fully under the control of the United States until U.S. forces from New Orleans surrounded the city on April 12, 1813, and demanded the surrender of the Spanish forces and the evacuation of Fort Charlotte (known as Fuerte Carlota to the Spanish). On January 11, 1861, Alabama seceded from the Union and for about one month, The Republic of Alabama ruled Mobile. Mobile was part of the Confederate States of America from February 8, 1861, to 1865. Mobile has remained a part of the United States since April 12, 1865.

The first documented account of a police force or police officer was in 1814. Major Wilbur Williams, Mobile Police Department (ret) began researching our history in the early 1990's and he discovered many dates and events in our long history. He was instrumental in obtaining photographs and a replica of the first known badge in our department's history. Tracing our history proves to be difficult because many records have been lost, and some are scant on information other than minutes of a meeting or a letter from one person to another. A portion of our records from 1865 to 1869 are found at the University of Alabama Special Collections Library archives. It is unknown when the archives came into possession of the records or from whom they were obtained.

Several years of research and collecting books, newspaper articles, combing the stored archives of the Department at Headquarters as well as the City Archives, public library, and interviews with former and current officers has led to the creation of this document.

It is impossible to relate every detail or story, or even every year in our history. This is a brief overview highlighting some of the interesting facts and occurrences in our Department's history. We claim a founding year of 1814, because that is the oldest official documentation that has been found that definitively states an officer was paid for conducting the duties of a police officer. From the founding of Mobile, to the early 1800s, there was a military garrison housed in Mobile at Fort Conde (Fort Charlotte under the English, Fuerte Carlota under the Spanish and again Fort Charlotte under the United States), and it is known that they oversaw order in the community, and the Governor of the Territory would hear cases. There were also judges appointed throughout the territory, so it is likely that some form of law enforcement officer was utilized. Until we can uncover some lost record that pre-dates April 1814, we will continue to recognize that year as the founding of the Mobile Police Department.

There is a report, documented in *Remember Mobile*, a book by Caldwell Delaney 1948 and 1969, that states in 1816, the City of Mobile was expanding. New construction was being conducted to the north of the old city limits in what would become the Orange Grove neighborhood. Additional expansion took place to the west, but to the south, the old fort was a barrier. The citizens began walking through the fort as a shortcut to the newly developed southern area, which irritated the soldiers. A fence was put up but quickly torn down by the citizens. The military commander put it back up and appealed to the city leaders to prevent their citizens from tearing it down again. The dispute continued between the military forces and the citizens over the right to walk through the fortification of Fort Charlotte to get to the south side of the city. As reported by Peter J. Hamilton in *Colonial Mobile* (pg. 477 published in 1897 and 1910), on May 17, 1817, the city government leaders wrote a letter to the commander of the fort stating that if the soldiers did not remove the barrier, they would order their police to do so by force. This was really an idle threat as it is also stated that at that time there was only one policeman on the force. That officer is named Lemuel Childress. It is noted in Hamilton that a few days after the letter was sent, the fence came down and Officer Childress was removed and replaced by Timothy McGrath. It was after this incident that new rules for the local government and the police were instituted. This disturbance set in motion the removal of soldiers from the fort and ultimately its destruction. In April 1818, Congress passed a resolution calling for the sale of the fort, and by March 1821 all soldiers, equipment, and stores had vacated the fort, moving to occupy Pensacola.

On April 20, 1940, the "Mobile Register" published an article that stated: In 1816 Mobile Police employed a full-time police officer who received $10 per month and half of the fines collected as a result of arrests made by him. (We always thought the fee system was outdated.) Two years later, an act of the Territorial Legislature authorized Mobile to appoint three police constables.

There have been thousands of men and women to serve on the Department since its inception. Some for a career, some for a few years before they moved on. Every person who has worn our badge and taken the oath of a police officer has left a mark on our Department. Each one of them has enough stories to write their own book of adventures, arrests, and observations. There is no way to name every officer or official who took part in any of the events that are recorded here. Their omission is not out of malice or due to a lack of research, but simply because it would render this document impossible to complete. This history is being recorded for them.

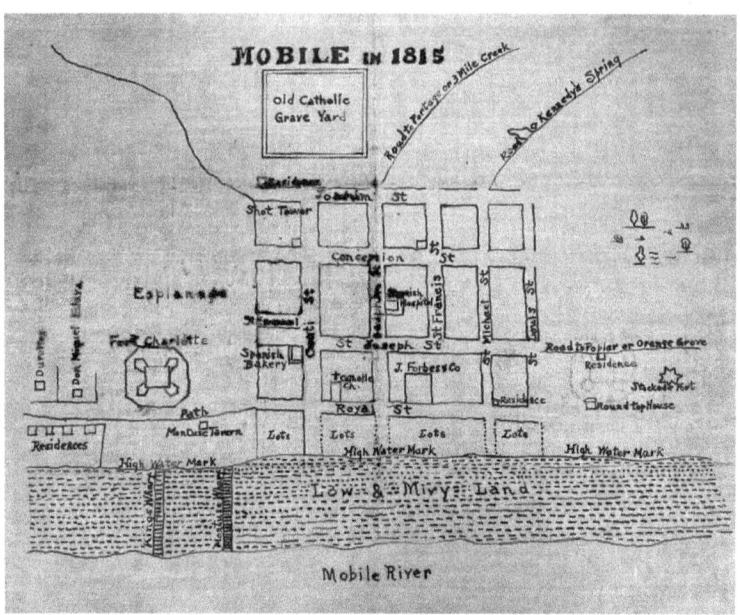

The 1815 Map of Mobile from the Minnie Mitchell Archive
Collection of the Mobile Historic Preservation Society.

The Early Years: 1814-1835

On April 7, 1814, the Town of Mobile Board of Aldermen approved the payment of fifty percent of a fine imposed on a citizen to Police Constable Pierre Laurendine.

On April 12, 1815, Teldea Nicola was elected Town Marshall for Mobile. His pay was $25 per year, plus fifty percent of all fines received by the Town. Nicola resigned on April 29, 1815, which prompted the Board of Aldermen to pay police officers $5 per month in addition to their part of the fines and fees collected by the Town.

On June 10, 1815, Reuben Reynolds was elected to serve as a police officer.

1816-1817, Lemuel Childress was the lone police officer.

On September 4, 1817, Timothy McGrath was appointed as a police officer.

On March 19, 1819, the Board of Aldermen approved paying officers $15 per month and eliminating the fifty percent payment of fines and fees collected by the Town.

On April 21, 1819, Daniel Moore was appointed as a police officer.

On December 11, 1819, Timm Merritt was appointed as a police officer.

On April 27, 1821, Charles Steel was appointed as a police officer.

Of Note: At some unknown point in time between March 19, 1819, and December 4, 1822, the pay for police officer was increased to $250 per year.

On December 4, 1822, John Soto was hired to be a police officer. On this date, the number of officers increased to three. With his appointment, the Board of Aldermen decreased the officer's annual salary from $250 to $200. On the same date, the Aldermen confirmed Daniel Steel and the first "Chief" of police in the Town of Mobile's history. The position is believed to be "Town Marshall."

On January 28, 1826, The Mayor and Aldermen of the City of Mobile passed an ordinance to establish a City Watch. It is as follows:

1826 CITY WATCH ORDINANCE

Ordinance 4
An Ordinance to establish a City Watch, and to regulate the duties of Watchmen
Passed 28 January 1826

Section 1. Be it ordained by the Mayor and Aldermen of the City of Mobile, That it shall be the duty of Police Officers to make out a roll or list of the names of all the free male persons over the age of sixteen years, now residing within the taxable limits of the said City; which list they shall from time to time correct, by adding the names of all free male persons who may hereafter become residents of said City, and shall have resided therein the term of ten days.

Sec. 2. Be it further ordained, That each and every person who may be enrolled as aforesaid, shall be liable to perform the duty of a Watchman in rotation; and in order to ascertain the persons who may be liable, from time to time, to perform such duty, the name of each person enrolled shall be put into a box, kept for that purpose, from which shall be drawn the names of so many as the Mayor and Aldermen, for the time being, shall deem necessary for Watchmen, each and every night; which drawing shall take place under the superintendence of the Mayor or any one of the Aldermen, for the time being; and in case the name of any person shall be drawn who may be absent from the City, or unable to perform the duty of a Watchman, by reason of sickness, the name of such person shall be returned to the box, and subject to be drawn again.

Sec. 3. Be it further ordained, That it shall be the duty of the Mayor or some one of the Aldermen, to make out a list of the names of persons who may be drawn for Watchmen, for each night, which list, signed by the Mayor or some one of the Aldermen, specifying the time and place for their attendance, it shall be the duty of the Police Officers to serve on each person, if to be found in the City, at least six hours before they are required to attend; and in case any person whose name may be drawn for a Watchman, and who may have been warned as aforesaid, shall neglect or refuse to attend and perform the duties of a Watchman, as hereinafter prescribed, or shall neglect to attend in due time, every person so offending shall forfeit and pay the sum of two dollars; Provided nevertheless, that any person who may be required as a Watchman, may be at liberty to furnish a good and faithful man in his stead.

Sec. 4. Be it further ordained, That the Mayor, or the Aldermen who may attend the drawing of the Watchmen as aforesaid, shall appoint the captain, who shall have command of the Watchmen and shall be authorized to direct their walks in such parts of the City as he may think proper; and shall take care that the Watchmen under his command are vigilant and attentive to their duty; that the City be, at no time, destitute of Watchmen walking in the streets during the night—and shall report, in the morning, to the Mayor, or some one of the Aldermen, every Watchmen who may fail to attend at the time and place he may have been warned, as aforesaid; and every Watchman who may have been guilty of any neglect of duty, disobedience of orders, or any rude, riotous or disorderly conduct during the night; and in case any Captain of the Watchmen, or any Watchman shall be guilty of a breach of any of the provisions of this ordinance, he or they so offending shall be liable to be fined not exceeding ten dollars.

Sec. 5. Be it further ordained, That any person who may be appointed Captain, agreeably to the fourth section of the ordinance, shall, on failure to attend and perform the duties of Captain of the Watchmen, as therein required, incur a penalty not exceeding five dollars: Provided always, that no person who has served as Captain, or who has paid a fine for the non-performance of the duties thereof, shall be liable to serve again as Watchman for the term of three months.

Sec. 6. Be it further ordained, That the Watchmen shall have full power and authority to stop and apprehend any suspicious person or persons, or any person or persons who may be in any manner guilty of disturbing the peace and good order of the City; and it shall be their duty to disperse all unreasonable, riotous, or disorderly meetings of slaves, or other persons, and may punish any slave found without a pass after the hour of nine o'clock at night, by whipping, not exceeding ten stripes; and every person apprehended may, at the discretion of the Captain of the Watchmen, be kept in the Watch-house, or may be confined in the City Prison, till an early hour in the morning, when it shall be his duty to report the person or persons in custody, to the Mayor, or some one of the Aldermen, to be dealt with as the ordinances of the City may require.

Sec. 7. Be it further ordained, That no ball, dance or assemblage of people of color shall hereafter be permitted within the City, unless the person or persons at whose house the same may be intended to be held, shall first have obtained a license from the Mayor, or one of the Aldermen, for that purpose; and that no such license shall be granted to extend beyond the hour of one o'clock at night; and it shall be the duty of the Watchmen to require such persons, at that hour, to retire to their dwellings, and in case of refusal they may be taken into custody as disorderly persons; and the person at whose house they were assembled, shall be deemed to have kept a disorderly house, and be liable to the penalties in such cases provided.

Sec. 8. Be it further ordained, That the fines and penalties contemplated by this ordinance, shall be sued for and recovered before the mayor, or any one of the Aldermen—one half whereof shall be for the use and benefit of the Police Officer for the time being, and the other half for the use of the City.

Sec. 9. Be it further ordained, that all ordinances and parts of ordinances, coming within the purview and meaning of this ordinance, be, and the same are hereby repealed.

On February 24, 1830, the Mayor and Aldermen passed an ordinance to establish a prison fee. It is as follows:

1830 ORDINANCE TO ESTABLISH PRISON FEE

An ordinance to establish a Prison Fee at the City Prison
Passed February 24, 1830

Section 1. Be it ordained by the Mayor and Aldermen of the City of Mobile, That from and after the passage of this ordinance it shall be the duty of the City Marshall to collect from all free persons confined in the City Prison, under any charge or pretext whatever, and before the discharge of any such free person, the sum of one dollar; and it shall also be the duty of the said Marshall to demand and receive from the owner or owners, employer or employers of each and every slave confined in the City Prison, under any charge or pretext whatever, and before such slave or slaves shall be discharged from custody, the like sum of one dollar.

Sec. 2. Be it further ordained, that all moneys collected under the provisions of this ordinance shall be paid into the Treasury for the use of the City.

Sec. 3. Be it further ordained, that it shall be the duty of the City Marshall to keep a book, in which shall be entered the name and description of every person hereafter confined in the City Prison, and the amount of prison fees collected, for which amount he shall account.

On April 27, 1830, one of the first documented citizen complaints on an officer can be found. Of note is the fact that the officer "pulled his sword" on the complainant. I can find no documentation indicating what the outcome of the complaint was.

1830 FALSE ARREST COMPLAINT

April 27, 1830

To the Mayor and Aldermen of the City of Mobile

Gentlemen,

On Sunday evening the 25th inst. whist on my way home, in company, with several gentlemen, I was met at St. Michael Street, by the Police Constable Mr. Soto and two other men, who were in company with him, when without cause, or provocation from me, he laid his hand on me, and said I must go to the Guard House. I felt no disposition to be treated in that manner, without making some resistance, although the only resistance made by myself, was to extricate myself, from him, which I did. He then drew is sword and called upon one of his associates to seize me, which was done, and I, was escorted to the Guard House.
I request that the testimony of David R. Hynes, Miles Crase, Roy Tankersley and G.W. Browne, be taken to testify to the truth of the above statement, and also the testimony of Col. Joseph Bates, whether he heard me make any noise, and the following, Mr. Curran, Mr. Watson, Mr. Cummins, and Mr. W. Shearer, to prove what Mr. Soto should of said a few nights previous to committing the outrage complaint.

Very Respectfully Yours
David Simpson

On April 13, 1835, the City of Mobile increased the

number of City Night Watch personnel, documented regulations, and identified uniforms:

1835 CITY WATCH AND UNIFORMS

Section 1. Be it ordained by the Mayor and Aldermen of the City of Mobile, and it is hereby ordained by the authority of the same, that the Night Watch shall hereafter consist of a Captain, a Lieutenant and twenty-three privates, and five additional privates whenever, in the opinion of the Mayor, the services of the City shall require such increase.

Sec. 2. Be it further ordained, That the officers and members of said Watch shall wear a uniform consisting in summer, of a blue cotton round jacket, single breast and standing collar, the same to be covered with red or yellow braid, or tape; white pantaloons, of linen or drilling, to be trimmed in like manner, and leather or Morocco caps. In the winter the jackets and pantaloons to be of blue cloth, trimmed as the summer dress, and gray or blue cloth cap; the Captain to wear a cotton knot on each shoulder and the Lieutenant one on the right, which uniform shall be furnished at the expense of the officers and men respectively, but to be made or procured under the direction of the Mayor, with such changes and alterations as he may think proper to suggest.

Sec. 3. And be it further ordained, That the Captain and Lieutenant shall each be armed with a white mounted sword, suspended by a black Morocco or leather belt, and a brace of side pistols, to be provided at their own proper expense; and the privates shall each be armed with a musket and bayonet, cartouche box, etc. and at all times to be provided with at least six rounds of ball cartridge, to be furnished at the expense of the City; but for the care, preservation and prompt return thereof, when required, they shall each be held responsible.

Sec. 4. And be it further ordained, that in addition to the ordinary duties required of the City Watch, it shall be their duty, under the command of the Captain and Lieutenant, to parade and drill at such place as the Mayor may direct, from eleven o'clock A.M. till one o'clock P.M., and from three to five o'clock P.M. every day; and moreover shall, at any hour of the day or night, in

(The remainder of this ordinance has not been located.)

City Registry and Census Highlights From 1837-1891

The following are names and dates that were found in archives regarding the makeup of the city and the police department. This list is not complete as the city registry and census forms for each year could not be located. The information listed is interesting in that it shows the frequency in changes of personnel in ranking positions.

In 1837:

Police Officers:
W.B. Akridge
S.J. Jones
John Morris

City Guard:
Captain Henry Etter
Lieutenant M. Callaghan
+ twenty-five men

Constables:
E. March
C. Steele
B. Herschy

In 1838:

Mayor: George Walton, annual salary was $2,500
Town Marshal: James H. Cocke, paid $2000 per year

Police Officers: paid $800 per year
North Ward- Jacob Cohen

Middle Ward- John B. Heard
South Ward- Thaddeus Seymour
West Ward- John Morris

In 1839:

Mayor: George Walton

Mobile City Marshal: T. M. Stockdell

Police Officers: Thaddeus Seymour
James Leonard
Charles C. Wilkins

City of Mobile Census: Population: 13,621
Whites: 8,594
Free people of color: 557
Slaves: 4,470

In 1842, there was a city marshal, and three deputy city marshals. Additionally, there was a captain and lieutenant of the City Guard and twenty privates elected by the Mayor, Aldermen, and Common Council. We have not found census numbers for 1842.

Mayor: Edward Hall

City Marshal: Jacob S. Cohen

Deputy City Marshals: U. T. Cleveland
Emanuel Alvarez
Warren Welch

City Guard: Captain B. Merino
Lt. William H. Torrens
Twenty unnamed privates.

In 1844:

Mayor: Charles Hoppin Salary $3000 per year
City Marshal: David Walker Salary $1500 per year
Deputy City Marshal: Charles T. Jenkins Salary $750 per year

City Guard:
Captain William G. Davy $750 per year
Lieutenant George Calloway $650 per year

Guard House Sentinel:
Christopher Thompson

In 1850:

Mayor: Charles C. Langdon
City Marshal: David Walker
Deputy Marshals: James Griffin
DeWitt Fuller

In 1855

Mayor: Charles C. Langdon
City Marshal: John Stuckey   Salary: $1,200 per year

Deputy City Marshals: DeWitt Fuller
Joseph Schollick,
Stephen Charpentier *(Would become the Chief of Police in 1858.)*
David Walker
Salary: $800 per year

In 1856

Mayor: Jones M. Withers
City Marshal: Henry Maury   Salary: $1,200 per year

Deputy City Marshals: Stephen Charpentier
Joseph Schollick
DeWitt Fuller
Salary: $800 per year

In 1859

Mayor: Jones M. Withers
Captain Stephen Charpentier, "Chief of Police"

Lieutenants: Joseph Schollick
R. W. Lewis
DeWitt Fuller

Sergeants: W. H. Kennedy
P. D. Carr
J. S. Whitney

In 1861

Chief of Police: Stephen Charpentier
Assistant Chiefs: J.S. Whitney
E. Girard
David L. Cummings
R.W. Lewis

Captain: P.D. Carr

Lieutenant: F.A. LeFevre

Sergeants: D. Fuller
J.M. Cleveland
J. Giddens
W.H. Kennedy
The Night Watchmen numbered fifty-four men.

In 1868 (January 1868 payroll)

Chief: C.A.R. Dimon
Captain of the Watch: Samuel Magill

Assistant Chief: John Bressingham (this is not the John Bressingham mentioned later)
        H. Milne
        John W. Schell
        Ovide Gregory (first Black assistant chief)

In 1869

Chief of Police: Colonel M.D. Wickersham
Assistant Chiefs: John Bressingham
        Henry Milne

In 1871

Chief of Police: Robert M. Quinn

Assistant Chiefs: S.A. Leonard
        Thomas McPhillips
        James Giddens
        Jesse T. Cain

In 1872

Chief of Police: William P. Barlow

In 1873

Chief of Police: Stephen Charpentier

Assistant Chiefs: M.C. Osborn
Henry Malone
A. Stykes

James Garrity

In 1875

Chief of Police: H. Milne

Assistant Chiefs: Thomas McPhillips
                James Garrity
                Michael F. Eldridge
                Edward Agerth
                R.W. Harris

In 1876

Chief of Police: T.L. Eastburn

In 1885

Chief of Police: Captain J.J. Crowley, bond $3000, annual salary $1200

Lieutenant: E. Rondeau, bond $1500, annual salary $750

Population (1880 census) 31,295
                      18,995 white
                      12,449 black

In 1890

Chief of Police: Richard Felder

Lieutenant of police: Charles E. Spencer

Sergeants of police: Eugene A. Eastburn, Joseph Hart, John McGuire
Special Officers: John Bressingham*, Thomas B. McGovern

Police officers: Henry J. Binzer, John W. Bridges, John M. Brown, H. Kenney Cleveland, Benj. P. Clonan, John Cummings, Jules Delhomme, Frank J. Demouy, Daniel P. Fletcher, Hugh Fox, Michael Gaynor, Lev J. D. Gibson, W. Duncan Hall, Chas. B. Harwell, Chas. R. Huggips, Leonard G. Jarvis, Albert H. Jennette, John King Jr., Jeremiah S. Lynch, Patrick J. Lynch, John McArdle, John McCarron, Mortimer L. McKean, Alza W. Moore, Dominick O'Connor, Richard H. Puckett, Edward T. Rondeau, William A. Ryan, Jas. Y. Shaw, John A. Tardy, Geo. J. Townsend, Peter Untreiner, William J. York.

John Bressingham was the longest serving Mobile Police Officer. He is on the payroll as a "special officer" in 1890, but his appointment date as a Police Officer is April 29, 1894. There will be a section dedicated to him as we move forward.

In 1891

Mayor: Joseph C. Rich

Chief of Police: Richard Felder

Standing Committee: Police/Guard House
Committee #5: Patrick J. Gibney, Chairman, J.T. Hawkins and P.W. Kelly

Lieutenant: Charles E. Spencer
Sergeants: Eugene A. Eastburn, Joseph Hart, John McGuire
Special Officers: John Bressingham, Thomas B. Mc Gowan
Secretary to Chief of Police: Augustus B. Roulston
Sanitary Officer: George W. Drago
Armorer: William H. Bancroft

Police Officers: Henry J. Bizner, John W. Bridges, John

W. Brown, H. Kenny Cleveland, Benjamin P. Clonan, John Cummings, Jules Delhomme, Frank J. Demouy, David P. Fletcher, Hugh Fox, Michael Gaynor, Levi D. Gibson, W. Duncan Hall, Charles, B. Harwell, Charles R. Huggins, Leonard G. Harvis, Albert H. Jennette, John King, Jr., Jeremiah S. Lynch, Patrick J. Lynch, John McArdle, John McCarron, Mortimer L. McKean, Alza W. Moore, Dominick O'Connor, Richard H. Puckett, Edward T. Rondeau, William A. Ryan, James Y. Shaw, John A. Tardy, George J. Townsend, Peter Untriener, William J. York

Supernumeraries: Joseph R. Adams, Robert Brady, Kyle Clound, Rodger Jones, John Joseph, John J. Leonard, Ferdinand Oberkirch, Albert M. Palmas

The First "Chief of Police"
Stephen David Charpentier

According to newspaper articles, Stephen D. Charpentier was born in August 1822 in New Orleans and came to Mobile as a young boy. He first appears in the Mobile County marriage records on May 24, 1847, when he married Sarah Horen.

In the book, *Craighead's Mobile* by Caldwell Delaney he writes that in 1827 a group of men who had fought for Napoleon Bonaparte and had departed France coming to Mobile after his fall, formed a military company called the Mobile Grenadiers. This military group was one of several in Mobile at that time. The Mobile Grenadiers were recorded as marching for the first time in uniform on March 20, 1828. They met at the northwest corner of Dauphin and Jackson at the home and tavern of one of the group founders, Jean Dragon. One of the officers was Lieutenant Pierre Charpentier, father of Stephen D. Charpentier. Stephen was named as a Company Marker along with John Julius Delchamps, both aged six to seven years old. Later in the book, it is written that Stephen Charpentier "proved to be an excellent police official, one of the best Mobile ever had."

There is no listing for either Stephen or Sarah Charpentier in the 1850 Mobile Census. We do find Stephen listed in the 1855 Mobile City Directory. He lists 29 Conti Street as his address and his occupation as Deputy City Marshal. The 29 Conti Street address was the address for the Mobile City Guard House. Again, in the 1856 edition of the Mobile City Directory, Charpentier is listed as a Deputy City Marshal without an address.

Jones M. Withers was elected Mayor in 1856, and it is believed that he began to institute changes in the Police Department that resulted in dropping the title "City Marshal" and instituting the title of "Chief of Police." The rank of the person holding the position as Chief was Captain, going back to the days when the person that oversaw the Night Watch was known as the Captain of the Watch. The rank of Captain for the Chief of Police remained in place for several more years before being dropped.

Beginning in 1858, the term Chief of Police was used for the first time. The name of the department was changed from Mobile City Marshals to Mobile City Police. The first chief was Stephen D. Charpentier, his rank was Captain, Chief of Police after being promoted from Deputy City Marshal. Stephen Charpentier replaced the town marshal who had been removed from office and who was engaged in an unsanctioned invasion of Nicaragua. This filibustering adventure was led by William Walker, and the group of adventurers sailed from Mobile in 1858.

In a collection of newspaper articles from 1858, we find an article indicating that Captain Charpentier, Chief of Police, was involved with another Police Officer, Private Lefevre, in the capture of two burglary suspects on Dauphin Street.

In 1859 during the continuation of the Withers' administration and with Charpentier as Chief of Police, other changes were noted in the Mobile Police Department. Organizational changes were made in the supervisory positions and the Department itself became known as Mobile City Police.

We find Stephen Charpentier in the 1860 census of Mobile along with the following family members. Stephen was listed as being 38 years of age and born in Louisiana (his death certificate from the Health Department states he was born in France). His occupation was listed as Chief of Police, and he lived on the Northwest corner of Conti Street and Bayou Street. His wife was listed as Sarah Charpentier, age 32, and born in Ireland. There was a daughter, Sarah Ann, age 11, born in Alabama; a daughter Lucy, age 9, born in Alabama; and a son, Stephen Jr., age 5, born in Alabama. In the 1870 census, Stephen is listed as having no job and his age was documented as 47. Sarah was listed as "keeping house," age 42. Sarah Ann. age 19, Lucy. age 15. and Stephen Jr.. age 13, all listed as "attending school." I can find no reason for the discrepancy in the children's ages from the 1860 to the 1870 census.

With all the changes being made during these years and the fact that a civil war seemed inevitable, we can assume that

Charpentier would have wanted his officers and their positions properly noted. We know that the Marshal's position had been known as Mobile City Marshal and that the Deputy's positions were noted as Mobile City Deputy Marshal. Once Charpentier was named Chief of Police, it officially became known as City of Mobile Police Chief and the department was called Mobile City Police.

We have documents stating that several police officers from the police department joined the Confederate States Army and fought at several major battles during the war.

Chief Stephen Charpentier was among that group and in fact organized a company, officially Company A, 2nd Battalion, Alabama Light Artillery, commonly known as Charpentier's Battery. The following were members of the Company:

STEPHEN D. CHARPENTIER, SR., CAPTAIN
JOHN M. JENKS, FIRST LIEUTENANT
LEMUEL H. GOODMAN, SECOND LIEUTENANT
WILLIAM J. LEE, THIRD LIEUTENANT
SAMUEL A. MILLER, FOURTH LIEUTENANT
DAVID D. HOREN, ORDERLY SERGEANT
JAMES CAHALL, QUARTERMASTER SERGEANT
SAMUEL CRENSHAW, FIRST SERGEANT
WILLIS NEWBOLD, SECOND SERGEANT
JOHN BRESSINGHAM, THIRD SERGEANT
FRANK MERVIN, FOURTH SERGEANT
ALEXANDER BOYDE, FIFTH SERGEANT
JERRY MANNING, SIXTH SERGEANT

ZEBULON LANDRUM, FIRST CORPORAL
E.R. NEWBOLD, SECOND CORPORAL
HUGH THOMPSON, THIRD CORPORAL
PATRICK CAIN, FOURTH CORPORAL
JAMES JAMMERSON, FIFTH CORPORAL
STEVEN JONES SIXTH CORPORAL

NATHAN COONE, FARRIER
AUGUST HARBURGER (OR HANGHBURG) BUGLER
HENRY ARNES, ARTIFICER

FREDERICK HODENMEYER, ARTIFICER
THOMAS ANDERSON, ARTIFICER

PRIVATES:

BANCROFT, JOHN (OR THOMAS)
BARRETT, THOMAS
BARRY, AUGUSTUS
BODGE, THOMAS
BOLTZ, JOHN
BRADLEY, JOHN
BRENNAN, BARNEY
BROWN, ALEX
BROWN, JOHN
BURKE, JOHN
CAROLTON, SIMS
CASSAGE, MARCUS
CONNERS, JAMES
CRONIN, PATRICK
CURRY, WILLIAM
DAVIDSON, JAMES
DENEHEY(OR DENBY), ANDREW
DOWLING, DENNIS
DOWLING, THOMAS
DOWLING, WILLIAM
DRISCOLL, TIMOTHY
ELLIS, THOMAS
EVANS, FRANK
EVERITT, GEORGE
FITZGERALD, ALEXANDER
FREEMAN, WILLIAM
GANNON, JOHN
GANO(OR GAND), RICHARD
GIBSON, CHARLES
GORDON, ALEXANDER
HALLISEY, MICHAEL
HAND, ANTHONY
HAYS, JOHN
HICKEY, JAMES 1ST
HICKEY, JAMES 2D.
HICKMAN, JOHN *(Awarded a memorial cross by the*

United Confederate Veterans in Mobile, 1-23-1910)
HIELER(OR HEITER), J. T.
HOFFMEYER, FREDERICK
HOPNATCH, HENRY
HORRIGAN, JOHN
HOUGH, JOHN
HULL, SAMUEL
HUMPHRIES, L.W.D.
JACKSON, HENRY
JACKSON, JOSEPH
JACKSON, WILLIAM
JONES, WILLIAM
KEATING, MICHAEL
KENNION, WILLIAM
KENNY, PATRICK
KING, WILLIAM
LANDRUM, BURNIS
LANDRUM, HENRY
LANE, GEORGE
LANEY, JOHN
LAVE, JAMES
LESLIE, JAMES
LEWIS, WILLIAM
MACKEY, JOHN
MANNING, JAMES
MARTIN, JAMES
MAXWELL, JOHN
MCCONNELL, JAMES
MCINTYRE, JAMES
MEEHAN(OR MECHAN), OWEN
MELTON, JOHN
MITCHELL, R. T.
MORAN, JOHN
MORGAN, JOHN
MURPHRIE, JOHN
MURPHRIE, WILLIAM
O'CONNOR, DOMINICK *passed away on January 6, 1911 in Mobile)*
O'DONNELL, JERRE
OVERSTREET, WILLIAM
PATTERSON, THOMAS

PLATTILLO, GEORGE *(buried in Confederate Rest, Magnolia Cemetery)*
REVERE(OR REVERIE), JOHN
ROBERTS, SOL.
ROLLINS, J.B.
ROLLS(OR ROLLE), JOHN
SCOTT, JOSEPH
SELBY, JOHN
SELBY, WILLIAM
SKELTON, WILLIAM
SMITH, RICHARD
STACK, THOMAS
TEVVICE, W.J.
TEW, JAMES
THOMAS, JEFF
THOMPSON, CHARLES
TREBLE, JOHN
TUCKER, JOSEPH
TUTTLE, WILLIAM*(passed away on March 25, 1910 in Mobile)*
VALENTINE, C.
VAUGHN, JAMES
WATTERS, LEAVEN
WEBSTER, HENRY
WESTCOTT, WILLIAM
WHITAKER, WILLIAM
WILLIAMS, LON H.
YOCKERS, JOHN
YOEST, ANDREW

The men and officers of this company were from Mobile and were organized and mustered in on October 17, 1861, for light artillery service. The battery remained in the defense of Mobile, being stationed around the city as well as being sent to Fort Morgan until June 1863, when it was sent to the Mississippi theater.

The company was assigned to Featherston's Brigade. The battery fought at Jackson, Mississippi, suffering light casualties. They were ordered to Dalton, Georgia, where it was in the first part of the relocation of the Army from Dalton in

February 1864.

The battery then reported to Selma, Alabama, to reequip and was attached as flying artillery under the command of General Nathan Bedford Forrest. While serving in Forrest's army, the unit fought at Rome, Georgia, in May 1864. During that series of battles at Resaca, the battery was struck by a shell that killed several of the horses assigned. After that battle, they returned to Selma, and the battery participated in the defense of that city until the army surrendered and the soldiers captured in April 1865.

Stephen Charpentier was wounded in the knee while in battle in Georgia and by November 1864, the wound was still causing significant pain while on horseback. On November 1, 1864, Charpentier wrote a letter to the War Department requesting to resign his commission due to the injury. A few days after he penned the letter, on November 7, 1864, the Mayor of Mobile, R.H. Slough, wrote a letter to James Seddon, the Secretary of War for the Confederate States of America, advocating for the acceptance of Charpentier's resignation. In Slough's letter, he states *"Captain S. Charpentier commanding Lt. Battery, having been wounded, and as far as I am able to judge is incompetent to do further military duty, having resigned his command, which I petition may be accepted for reason assigned and for the purpose of my appointing him Chief of Police a position long held by him previous to the wars, and in addition to the competency in that capacity, he will be able to organize the Police into a well-disciplined military company to act in that capacity in times of necessity, as well as discharging the duties of police."*

When Stephen returned from the War, he returned to his position as Chief of Police and remained in that position until May 22, 1867. Congress had instituted Military Reconstruction on May 2, 1867, and Major General John Pope was in charge. On May 22, 1867, Pope ordered the removal of Jones M. Withers as Mayor and Stephen Charpentier as Chief of Police.

Major General Pope appointed General Charles Augustus Ropes Dimon as Chief of Police. On May 27, 1867, Dimon wrote a letter to the new Mayor, Gustavus Horton, requesting the Department be increased in numbers. At that time, the Day Force consisted of three sergeants, three corporals, and twenty privates. It was recommended that the number be increased to forty privates. The Night Force consisted of four sergeants, four corporals, and sixty privates. Dimon recommended the number of privates be increased to one hundred. In his justification, he stated that due to the increased size of the city and the lack of personnel, nearly twenty-five percent of the city lacked adequate police coverage on both day and night shifts. By the end of June, several hundred letters of application were received from men who wished to be appointed to the police department. Most of these applications were from former U.S. soldiers who had fought in the war. Applications came from as far as New Jersey and Missouri. It should be noted that the shortage in officers was due to the new Mayor firing nineteen officers the first week of his tenure. Over the next several months, Horton fired several more officers due to their "rebel" allegiances. Horton had refused to serve on the Confederate side during the war and his new position allowed him to reorganize the "rebel department."

Several months after being installed as Chief of Police. General Dimon received a shipment of new police uniforms that had been ordered by Chief Charpentier. When the uniforms were delivered, it was eventually decided to destroy the new uniforms during a public display in Bienville Square. Even though Chief Charpentier had ordered the new uniforms from a tailor in New York, and they were made exactly the same as Central Park Police, now NYPD, they were gray in color and General Dimon, and Major General Pope were furious. The new uniforms were burned at noon on the appointed day in the middle of Bienville Square.

Stephen Charpentier was employed in various occupations during the following years and on January 3, 1873, he again was appointed Chief of Police. He remained in that position for one year and then returned to private employment for the remainder of his life.

Chief Charpentier died on January 4, 1895. His death certificate states that he died of "congestion of lungs" and that he had been ill for ten days. He died at Number 7 St. Emanuel Street. According to a published report in the "Souvenir History of Mobile Police and Fire" in 1902, when discussing Charpentier's death, it stated, "the funeral was the occasion of one of the most general expressions of esteem ever tendered a

Confederate soldier and former police officer." It is odd that this publication, made in 1902 would have his date of death incorrect by several years. There also does not appear to be any notices in the newspaper about his actual death, other than a newspaper funeral notice that states: CHARPENTIER-Died January 4, 1895, at 2:20 p.m. STEPHEN P. CHARPENTIER, in the seventy-second year of his age. The friends of the family are requested to attend his funeral from the Cathedral SUNDAY AFTERNOON at two o'clock. It should also be noted that the funeral notice had his middle initial listed as "P" instead of "D."

There was an article published in the Montgomery, Alabama, "Daily Advertiser," dated Thursday, January 3, 1895, that states: **Capt. Charpentier Dangerously Ill-** Mobile, Jan 2, (Special) Capt. Stephen Charpentier is lying critically ill at his home on St. Edmunds [sic, St. Emanuel] Street, and his physicians fear he cannot live through the night. He is one of the best known of the old residents of Mobile, having come to this city when a boy from New Orleans, where he was born in August 1822. He has served as Chief of Police of Mobile and was a gallant Confederate soldier, being Captain of the famous Charpentier Battery.

Articles about Stephen Charpentier's Civil War artillery company indicate he was well regarded as a leader of men. One Confederate soldier, buried in Confederate Rest at Magnolia Cemetery, has Charpentier's Battery noted on his tombstone.

Further research shows that he was buried in Catholic Cemetery, and the *1962 Tombstone Inscriptions Catholic Cemetery* book published by Mobile Genealogical Society has him listed as being buried in Section XXX, Lot 7, with no marked grave.

Working with the head of Catholic Cemetery, I was provided documents that stated Stephen Charpentier was buried there in 1895; a Sarah A Charpentier (his daughter Sarah Ann) was buried there in 1883; and Sarah H. Charpentier (his wife) was buried there in 1900. I was provided documents from 1970 that indicated the unmarked concrete slabs over the graves had broken and collapsed, and the brick wall surrounding Lot 7 was falling over. Due to the deterioration of the slabs and wall, they were removed. The name plate that had been on the step leading into Lot 7 with S. Charpentier engraved on it was left on the lot.

On October 24, 2024, I took Mobile police officers from the Homeland Security Unit with their ground penetrating radar and officers from the Identification Unit to the grave site. We were able to determine the orientation of the graves in Lot 7 and verify there were three graves. There were no markings other than the engraved step mentioned above. I called retired Major Wilbur Williams, and he met us at the site. Plans were made to obtain a memorial marker for our first Chief of Police, recognizing his service as well as recognizing his wife and daughter.

I was also able to locate his descendants. Stephen's son, Stephen II, had moved to St. Louis, Missouri, in the late 1800s and married. He had a son, Stephen III, who was ten years old when Stephen II passed away in 1896. After much research, the descendants of Chief Charpentier were found in Texas and Missouri. When I reached out to the family, they were excited to hear about their grandfather. They had searched their genealogy and could only go as far as Stephen III, believing he was an orphan. Sarah Ann had no descendants. Lucy died one month before her mother in 1900, also leaving no descendants.

On December 13, 2024, I was able to purchase a stone memorial marker for Chief Charpentier. Ascencion Funeral Home offered to sell the marker at cost, and with assistance from Lieutenant (retired) Kay Taylor, Freddie Wheeler, and John Weichman, the marker was paid for in full and ordered.

On Friday, February 21, 2025, a memorial dedication ceremony was held at Catholic Cemetery to honor Stephen Charpentier as the first Chief of Police. The memorial stone was engraved with his information as well as Sarah Horen and Sarah Ann's. The ceremony was well attended, and the Mobile Police Department videographer documented the event so the family of Stephen Charpentier could view the ceremony.

No known photographs of Stephen Charpentier can be found.

Memorial service for Chief Charpentier, Catholic Cemetery,
February 21, 2025.

Chiefs of Police

As noted previously, the City of Mobile had officers and constables dating to 1814, but there was no "Chief of Police" designated. In the early years of the Department, the officers answered to ward commissioners. The following are the known Town Marshals and the Chiefs of Police. Inside Police Headquarters, the photographs of Chiefs of Police line the staff hallway. The first picture on the wall is of Mobile's second police chief, Chief Dimon, as no known photograph of Chief Charpentier exists. In addition to Chief Charpentier, several other portraits of men who served as Chief of Police are missing from the wall, and those are noted in these pages.

April 12, 1815-April 29, 1815
Teldea Nicola   Town Marshal
(There was no other Chief or Marshal from the time of Nicola's resignation to December 4, 1822.)

December 4, 1822- ?
Daniel Steel   Town Marshal

1838-1839
James H. Cocke   Town Marshal

1839-1842
T.M Stockdell   Town Marshal

1842-1844
Jacob S. Cohen   Town Marshal

1844-1850
David Walker   Town Marshal

December 28, 1853
John T. Webb   Town Marshal

December 27, 1854
John Stuckey   Town Marshal

December 26, 1855
Harry Maury   Town Marshal

Dec 27, 1855-Jan 8, 1856
John Stuckey   Town Marshal

Jan 9, 1856-Jan 22, 1858
Harry Maury   Town Marshal

Beginning in 1858, the term Chief of Police was used for the first time. The name of the Department was changed from Mobile City Marshals to Mobile City Police. And as mentioned before, the first chief was Stephen D. Charpentier. His rank was Captain, Chief of Police.

It is noteworthy that at the outbreak of the Civil War, Charpentier and several officers left to fight. See articles attached. During his absence 1861-1865, Robert T. Chamberlain headed the department. Charpentier and the mayor were dismissed from office in 1867.

During Reconstruction, there were multiple references to police chiefs. There are documents that indicate one person was Chief, when another document may support another person also being chief at the same time. A newspaper article stored at the Special Collections Library at the University of Alabama, dated February 22, 1870, gives a glimpse into this. It states: *Mr. McPhillips, acting as Chief of Police, under ex-mayor Price, surrendered the guardhouse, whereupon the Acting Mayor called for Mr. Bressingham, who immediately appeared, and was directed by Dr. Coalee to take charge in the capacity of temporary Chief of the police force. Mr. Bressingham assumed this duty and proceeded to reorganize the police force. And that ended the disagreeable and unpleasant struggle which has existed, much to the distaste of the people for the past week, as to who was mayor. The question now being settled, we trust that quiet, to a somewhat disturbed city, will be speedily restored.*

The name McPhillips and Bressingham are not included in the list of police chiefs. Bressingham was an assistant chief as noted in the city records. I can find no further information on McPhillips

During the Reconstruction period after the War Between the States, General Pope was assigned as the Commander of the Region. He removed duly elected politicians and replaced them with his appointees. He removed the police chief and appointed Colonel Charles Dimon. There is reference to a Colonel W.D. Wickersham being the Chief of Police, but as noted, there are some discrepancies in the timeline. Here is the most accurate list of Chiefs of Police as of the writing of this book.

1858-May 22, 1867
Stephen D. Charpentier   First Chief of Police

May 22, 1867- June 1869
Col. Charles A.P. Dimon   (photo at HQ)
*Appointed by Gen. John Pope.

1869- Feb 1871*
Col. W.D. Wickersham   Listed as Chief (photo at HQ), According to the book, *Highlights of 100 years in Mobile, 1865-1965* by the First National Bank of Mobile, on May 11, 1866, the Mayor of Mobile, J.M. Withers, and the Board of Aldermen donated three acres of land to the Federal Government to bury the United States soldiers. That was done at the request of Colonel W.D. Wickersham, the chief of the Quartermaster Department of Alabama. The land donated is located on Virginia Street at Magnolia Cemetery.

1870-?
W.W.D. Turner   (no photo at HQ)
We have a letter from Turner to the mayor dated March 10, 1870 as Chief at the end of the chapter.

1871-1872
Robert Quinn   (no photo at HQ)

Jan 2, 1872-1874 [sic]
William Barlow   (photo at HQ)
Listed in HQ as chief from 1872-1874, but we know that
Stephen D. Charpentier was again chief from 1873-1874.

1873-1874
Stephen D. Charpentier   (no photo at HQ)

1875-1876
H. Milne   (no photo at HQ)

1876-1877
Theodore L. Eastburn   (no photo at HQ)

1879
Colonel E.M. Underhill   (no photo at HQ)
Provisionally appointed by the commissioners.

1879-1885
William H. Williamson   (no photo at HQ)

March 18, 1885- March 1889
Captain J.J. Crowley   (no photo at HQ)
Bond $3000, annual salary $1200

March 1889-March 1890
H.H. Slatter   (no photo at HQ)

March 1890-March 28, 1894
Richard Felder   (no photo at HQ)

March 1894-March 1897
Peter Burke   (photo at HQ)

March 1897-March 1903
C. Walter Soost   (photo at HQ)

March 16, 1903-March 1905
John Case   (no photo at HQ)

March 1905-March 1909
Edward T. Rondeau   (photo at HQ)
After his tenure as chief of police, Edward Rondeau remained on the police department. He was made Chief of Detectives, a position he held until his death on July 25, 1920.

April 1909-June 1912
Vincent A. Giblin   (photo at HQ)
He is listed this way on his photo at HQ. See the Frank Crenshaw letter at the end of this chapter.

June 1912-Oct 1914 [sic]
Walter Walsh   (photo at HQ)
I can find no record of Walsh, other than a note in a 1918 article that indicates he was a Chief. He may have been Chief briefly from June 1912. His tenure was short enough that he did not obtain a new letterhead with his name on it. (See the Crenshaw note in the next listing.) Walsh should be credited with the Chief's tenure as June 1912- Oct 1912.

Oct 1912-Oct 1915 [sic]
Frank W. Crenshaw   (photo at HQ)
I have a letter from Crenshaw to Mayor Schwarz dated May 13, 1913. (See Frank Crenshaw letter below.) This is written on police letterhead with V.A. Giblin's name crossed out and it is signed Chief F.W. Crenshaw.
An article from the "Mobile News Item" paper dated October 26, 1913 states that Frank W. Crenshaw has been the head of the department since October 7, 1912. It appears that Crenshaw was chief from then until -October 1915.

Oct 1915-Dec 1917
Gilbert M. Van Liew   (missing photo at HQ) I have his written oath of office dated October 21, 1915. See the final letter section at the end of this chapter.

Dec 1917-Dec 1923

Patrick O'Shaughnessy   (photo at HQ)

O'Shaughnessy was indicted and arrested by the Federal government for running illegal liquor. He was convicted and sentenced to two years but won a reversal on appeal. His new trial was set for April 1928. He was beaten on February 2, 1928, at South Lawrence between Canal Street and Palmetto Street by J.B and Murrell Tait. He died on February 24, 1928, from his injuries.

Dec 1923-Dec 1924

Jesse Hogan   (photo at HQ)

Dec 1924-May 1938

Warren Burch   (photo at HQ)

May 1938-Oct 1941

Emory Warren   (photo at HQ)

Oct 1941-Oct 1961

Dudley McFadyen   (photo at HQ)

Oct 1961-July 1963

Talley Rollings   (photo at HQ)

July 1963-Dec 1970

James Robinson   (photo at HQ)

Dec 1970-Aug 1974

Edward McLean   (photo at HQ)

Aug 1974-Jan 1981

Donald Riddle   (photo at HQ)

Jan 1981-April 1981

James A. Botta and Walter G. Burch served intermittently as acting chiefs

Apr 1981-Jan 1984

Winston "Boots" Orr   (photo at HQ)

Jan 1984-Jan 1985   (photo at HQ)
Robert Larison

Jan 1985-Nov 1989   (photo at HQ)
William Mingus

Feb 1990-June 1996   (photo at HQ)
Harold Johnson

Oct 1996-Mar 2006   (photo at HQ)
Samuel Cochran

July 2006-Oct 2009   (photo at HQ)
Phillip Garrett

Oct 2009-Aug 2010
Lester Hargrove, Interim, no photo

Aug   2010-Nov   2013 (photo at HQ)
Micheal T. Williams

Nov 2013-Apr 2017   (photo at HQ)
James H. Barber

Apr 2017-Apr 2021   (photo at HQ)
Lawrence Battiste

Apr 2021-Oct 2021
Roy Hodge, Interim, no photo

Oct 2021-Apr 2024   (photo at HQ)
Paul O. Prine

Apr 2024-Sept 2024
William (Randy) Jackson, Interim, no photo

Sept 2024-current as of publication
William (Randy) Jackson

The Chief W.W.D. Turner letter, March 1870,

six pages

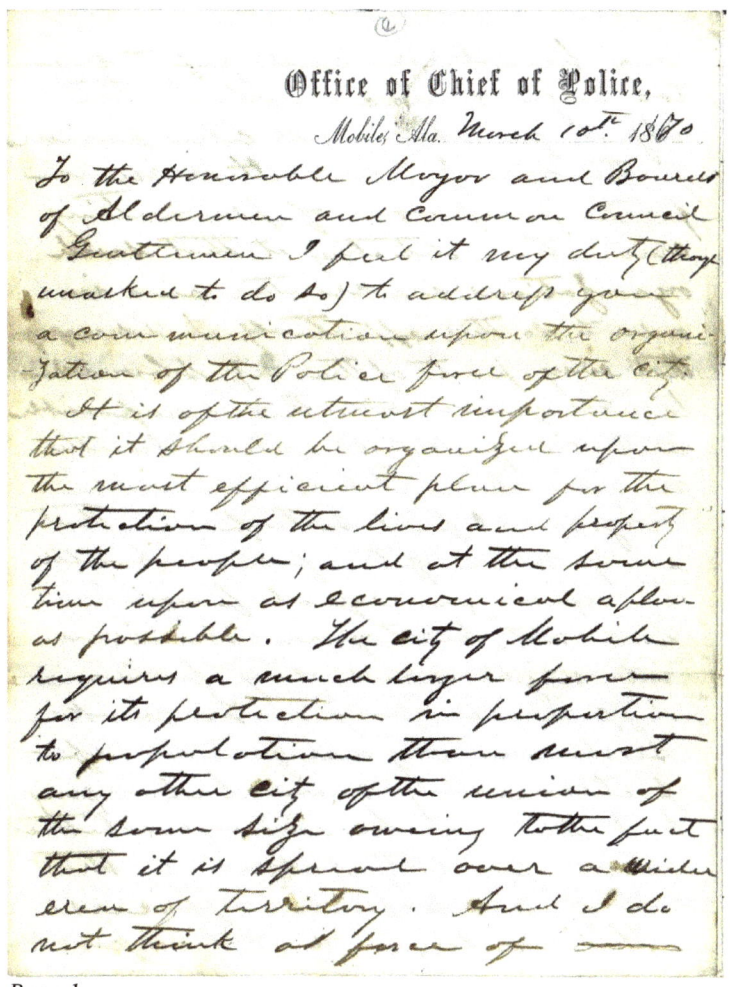

Page 1

one hundred and fifty men too large to accomplish the object for which all cities provides for this organization. It is more for the purpose of preventing crime than detecting it that such organizations are created and in order to do this effectually it is necessary that every part of the city should be well guarded - this is impossible in the city of Mobile with a smaller number than I have named.

Again I feel satisfied that every man of the force should be upon an equal footing and not as heretofore divided into night and day police - differing in pay. To make such an organization effective every man belonging to it should be always whether on or off duty subject to the call of his superior officers.

This would be next to impossible

their number of "Specials" sworn
in for the occasion. I have
therefore taken the liberty of dividing
the force under my command
into two equal divisions each
under the immediate command
of a competent officer who is held
responsible for the efficiency of
division. And although the force
is so small when the necessary "de-
Tails" have been as to leave me
only about forty men for "beat"
and "patrol" duty yet I am of the
opinion short as has been the
experiment that the force is
much more effective than under
the old plan. As it is the two
Divisions relieve each other
both officers and privates
every twelve hours and in such
a manner as to give each one

Page 3

43

Six hours sleep at night and an equal rest during the day – and my own experience is that an hour's sleep at night will refresh the system more than two hours in the day time. And besides this division of the force will enable the officers during the day to have a large reserve force at the Guard House ready at a moment's notice for active duty

Again in this way the officers are better enabled to have a control of the force, than if they were all scattered over the city thereby necessitating a length of time to get them together at the required locality. An organization as above suggested requires equal duty from every man on the force and when they only have six hours night service to perform it is but right they should while on duty be held to a strict requirement

Page 4

a living for themselves and
families and at the same
time be of service to the public
The foregoing reflections
have hastily suggested themselves
to my mind amid a variety of
conflicting duties which has pre
vented much thought upon the
subject but such as they are
I submit them for what they
are worth. I feel sure that
the numbers suggested is not out
of proportion either to the popu
lation or Territory of the city nor
do I believe the compensation
to be above a minimum price
I submit this communica-
tion with deference to your
better judgements and trust
it may be received and acted
upon in the same spirit
it is submitted, and that what
ever seems good in it may be
adopted and whatever bad

Page 5

45

rejected. I have but one object in view in submitting it and that is the welfare, peace, law, and order, of the City. If this end can be in your judgements accomplished with a smaller force than I have suggested of course it ought to be done.

But if it can not it strikes me a few hundred dollars should not be allowed in a city of so much importance to stand in the way of a complete protection of the lives and property of its people.

Respectfully
W. W. Turner
Chief of Police

Page 6, final

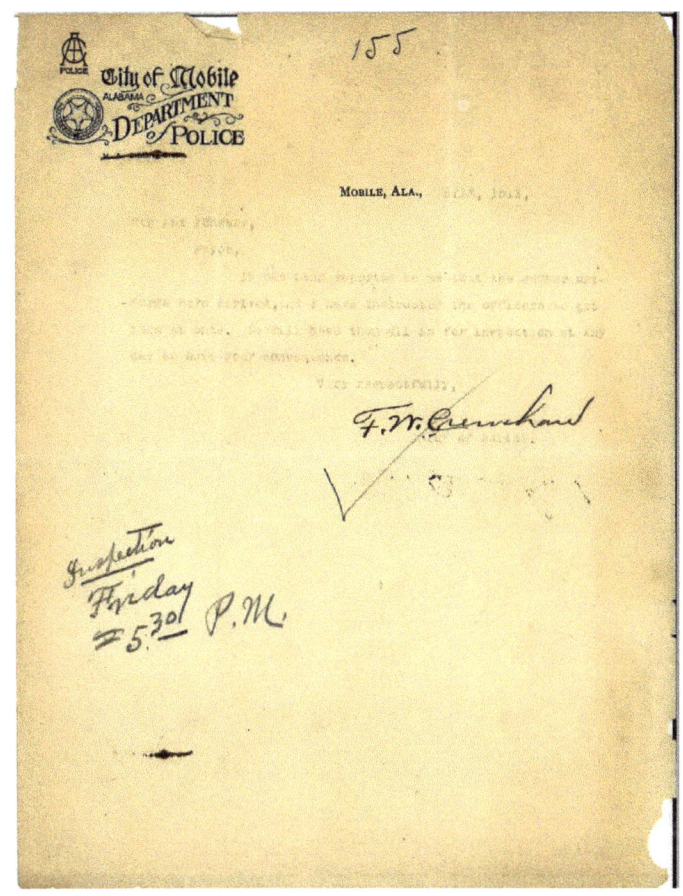

Chief Gilbert M. Van Liew Oath of Office
October 21, 1915

671

I, Gilbert M. Van Liew, who was elected chief of the police department of the City of Mobile by the Board of Commissioners of said City, on Tuesday, October 19th, 1915, by a majority vote of said Board, do hereby make oath and solemnly swear that I am eligible for the said office and will execute the duties of the same according to my best knowledge and belief; I further swear that I will support and maintain the Constitution and laws of the State of Alabama and of the United States. In token whereof I have set my hand to this oath on this the 21st, day of October, 1915.

State of Alabama }

Mobile County. }

      Before me, Pat J. Lyons, Mayor of the City of Mobile and member of the Commission of said City, personally appeared on this the 21st day of October, 1915, Gilbert M. Van Liew, to me known, and made and subscribed to the above written, his official oath as chief of police of the City of Mobile.

      Subscribed and sworn to before me this, the 21st day of October, 1915.

                    Mayor.

Chief Charles Walter Soost

Chief Charles Walter Soost was Chief of Police from March 1897 to March 1903. Soost was a progressive chief and under his leadership, the police department grew and became more professional.

Charles Walter Soost was born in Mobile on July 29, 1860. It can be said that his journey to the position of Chief of Police took a strange path. He was never a police officer in any capacity before he was appointed Chief of Police by Mayor J.C. Bush in March 1897.

Soost was an apprentice machinist at Kling's Foundry and then at the Louisville and Nashville Railroad shops. He became a volunteer firefighter at Washington Steam Fire Company Number 8. While serving on the volunteer fire department, he was elected to several positions including Assistant Chief Engineer. In early 1888, the City of Mobile abolished the volunteer fire departments and formed the Mobile Fire Department. Soost was hired by the City in the same position he had been at the Washington Steam Fire Company.

Under Soost's leadership, the old volunteer department was reorganized into a benevolent association. They sold the horses and equipment, taking those funds to assist the sick and to help pay for funerals of former volunteers and family.

After about three years of being a paid Assistant Chief on the Fire Department, Soost was appointed Chief of Police. I am sure that there was some grumbling amongst the officers. There has always been competition and rivalry between police and firefighters, but the rivalry and distrust between the two groups in Mobile in the late 1890s would have been fierce.

Before the city abolished the volunteer firefighters and formed a paid department, the volunteers had ruled the politics of the city. It was said that if you were a volunteer firefighter, you would be untouchable in regard to arrests or citations. There were several instances where the police and volunteers engaged in violent encounters. It should be noted that it wasn't only between the police and volunteers, but between volunteer companies and each other. They would fight each other if they responded to the same calls.

Once on the job, it didn't take long for the officers to realize they had a quality leader at the helm. Soost had developed a reputation as a strict disciplinarian in the volunteer fire department, driving out volunteers who brought discredit to the group. He brought that to the police department as well. Standards were implemented and officers were held to it. Equipment was upgraded and the department grew with the city.

Prior to Chief Soost, officers were often hired because of personal friendships or political favor. Those appointments changed, and officers started being hired for their ability. The Department was understaffed during his tenure, but with each passing year, the city council approved additional funding for new hires and equipment. With this new professionalism came acclaim. Chief Soost and the Department were praised locally and nationally for their control of the panic of the city due to a yellow fever outbreak in 1897, as well as their handling of the quarantines in 1899 and 1900 for yellow fever epidemics. Entire books could be written about the yellow fever epidemics that occurred in Mobile during the last few years of the 19th century. There were so many deaths that new cemeteries had to be built. Chief Soost and the Police Department handled this panic with professionalism and grace.

Under Chief Soost's leadership, the department became much more efficient in how the officers conducted business. Despite being short-handed for a city of 52,000 residents, the officers continued to make arrests, issue citations, and recover stolen property. Their duties continued to grow with the city and with the increased trade at the docks and along the railroads. From a report in 1902, we learn that the number of arrests in 1898 was 3,438; in 1899 it was 3,681; in 1900 it rose to 4,414; and in 1901 it was 5,200. Fines collected increased from $5,177.61 in 1898 to $9,354.35 in 1901. Officers became more efficient in investigating crimes as well. In 1898, they recovered $2,626 in stolen property; by 1901 it increased to $5,087; and by mid-1902, they had recovered $9,952. These efforts and successes led the city council to provide additional funding for the department. The Police budget increased from $33,482.91 in 1898 to $48,004.14 in 1901.

In the mid-1880s, twenty Gamewell Call System boxes had been placed in locations throughout the city. They had some benefit, but the Department lacked officers and equipment to make them truly efficient. With the improvements in the Department's professionalism and increased budget noted above, new officers and equipment such as paddy wagons were procured. The old call boxes were used when an officer needed assistance, but due to a lack of officers and wagons, it often fell to the officer to walk a disorderly arrestee to the station. The officer would have to be near the call box to hear it if headquarters was calling them. In 1901, the city installed new signal and telephone lines which, under the urging and advocacy of Chief Soost, led to an improved call box system. This new call box system could now connect headquarters with officers on the street with telephone capability. The supervisor of Mobile Electrical Lighting Company, Mr. S.C. Schaffner, invented an upgrade to these call boxes. With his invention, the boxes would sound an alarm as well as illuminate a light above the box. The light would stay lit and bell would ring until the officer opened the box and turned it off. At night, the streetlight would extinguish when the call-box light was activated, which enhanced the call-box light. This upgraded technology improved the efficiency of the department.

It can be said that Chief Charles Walter Soost laid the foundation for a professional, well- trained, well-equipped, and disciplined police department. Though the city was several years away from establishing a Civil Service classification or Personnel Board, the professionalism and efficiency displayed by the officers under Soost's leadership kept the Department from sliding back into political appointments and dismissals.

Chief Soost left the department in March of 1903 and passed away on January 20, 1933.

1900 Annual Report

In March 1900 Chief Soost completed his annual report to the Mayor and Council of Mobile. At that time, the fiscal year ended in March instead of October as it does today. The report has been reproduced, as written by Chief Soost, below as it shows the progressive style of improving the police department that Chief Soost embodied.

Mobile, March 19th-1900

To the Honorable Mayor, and General Council of the City of Mobile.

Gentlemen:

I have the honor to submit my third annual report, and in so doing to respectfully suggest such additions and improvement in the service, as experience has demonstrated to be necessary and useful in the way of needed improvements, I can recommend none more highly than the providing of this department with telephone attachments to the police signal system: this is in the hands of the City Electrician, can be added at small cost and will make this branch of the service perfect.

From daily experience I am convinced that it will not only improve the efficiency of the force by putting every quarter of the city in close touch with the office at all hours, but aid us in finding an officer in a comparatively short time, citizens living in the vicinity of the boxes can be furnished with keys, thereby being in instant communication with police headquarters whether an officer be near or not.

I believe the adoption of the above will in the interest of the public generally and will prove of vast importance to this department.

Our city is increasing both in wealth and inhabitants, and such modern improvement as this will not only increase the efficiency of this department but put it on a par with other police departments in the United States.

BERTILLION SYSTEM

This system of measuring and identifying criminals has been adopted by a large number of cities and has proved of great benefit in locating and securing previous records of criminals. Each city is assessed according to population, and it has been demonstrated beyond all measure of doubt, that a man once measured cannot escape detection; this work can be added to the regular duties of the detective department and maintained at a cost of not more that Thow hundred dollars, which would include assessments and purchasing apparatus.

DETECTIVE SERVICE

I take pleasure in complementing this important branch of the department, for excellent service rendered and untiring efforts on the part of its members in arresting the many criminals of more or less repute. Some of these captures, still fresh in the minds of the public, have attracted the attention of the best known police authorities, from when a number of complementary letters of praise and commendation has been received.

I therefore take pleasure in inviting your special attention to their report of arrests and recovering stolen property, it being far in excess of any previous year.

CHARITY

Aside from the criminal business, the police has been called upon to perform unusually large amount of miscellaneous work, of which none was entered into with more zeal by the officers than the opportunity to distribute Charity among the poor and destitute.

This system of relief has been organized and successfully handled by this department, and particularly was it noticeable during the extreme cold weather, through the well known generosity of the Honor Mayor Bush, this department was furnished with two car loads of coal and one of wood, which, through the kindness of Cap't A.C. Danner, of the Mobile Coal Co, and Messers Galliard and Johnston, was promptly delivered free of charge to a number of our deserving poor, among whom were a number of families who would have suffered in silence rather than ask assistance.

SANITARY

The security of life and property during the past year shows earnest and diligent effort of each and every member of the force.

Their work from a sanitary stand-point, has kept the city in excellent condition, and while unable to furnish a detailed report of inspections and communications as heretofore, it will no doubt be found among the Health Reports, be at the request of the City Health officer, _____ _____ on _____ work were ordered to report directly to him.

Still, I can refer with pride at the efficient services and interest of the department in all manners concerning the health of the City of Mobile.

QUARANTINE

This was found necessary to be ordered by the Board of Health against Key West, Fla on Sep't 1st 1899 on Sep't

2nd it was declared against New Orleans, La, and immediate action taken by meeting train #2 at midnight allowing no passengers from that city to leave the train.

The service was taken charge of State Health officer Sanders, and acting under his orders, Inspectors were placed on train, relay-camp established, dirt roads guarded and water ways protected on Mississippi Sound and Grant's Pass and Dauphin Island, daily reports being made at this office.

On Sep't 19th all branches of quarantine were transferred to the Marine Hospital Service, and to the untiring efforts of the Health authorities and the hearty co-operation of the Rail-road officials, the splendid result were again obtained as in 1898, an no case of fever succeeded in gaining entrance into Mobile, Quarantine being officially raised on Saturday, November 4th.

SMALL-POX

The opportunities of members of this department have aided materially in keeping advised the City and County Health officers of suspicious cases of sickness, while the maintenance of guards, furnishing of supplies and delivery of sick to the Pest-House, have been promptly attended to through this department, acting under the advise and orders of the City and County Health officers.

The dis-infecting of clothing and fumigation of houses has been handled in an excellent manner by the Sanitary officer, to whose attached report I invite your attention.

The Pest-House was opened on December 15th 1899 being still in use at present writing, the number of patients treated and Itemized Statement of expenses as incurred from this office will be found in Exhibit "_".

PRISON LABOR

The prisoners and work done by them have been under the supervision of this department.

They have performed during the year, 7,160 days of labor, distributed as ordered from time to time by the Mayor, on Streets, Cemeteries, Etc, shown in Exhibit "_".

At no time was this service better utilized than during the summer months in cleaning and dis-infecting yards and alleys, and the Comparative report shows the cost of feeding to be about the same as the last two years, an average of Six cents per day.

In conclusion I beg leave to say that considerable individual and collective pride has been secured by drilling, and while of minor importance to the suppression of crime, it has enabled us to make proper presentation to our superiors and the public, both of whom I am satisfied appreciate the efforts and appearance of the force under whose protection they place themselves and their property.

I would be ungrateful were I to close this report without extending my thanks to the Lieutenants, Sergeants, Detectives, and each patrolman, not forgetting my Clerk, for their close attention to orders, and their promptness in seeing that they are obeyed, together with their gentlemanly behavior on all occasions.

I also wish to express my thanks to his Honor, the Mayor for the cordial support he has given me in maintaining discipline and improving the force, to the members of the police committee and members of the General Council, and also the heads of department, for their many courtesies and cordial co-operation in all my efforts to advance the welfare of the people.

I am reminded in concluding this report of the necessity of inviting your special attention to a comparative statement of the past three years, and to the different attached reports showing in detail the many and varied duties pertaining to this department.

Very respectfully
(signed) C.W. Soost
Chief of Police

The Attached Reports were as follows.

COMPARATIVE STATEMENT FOR THE YEARS ENDING MARCH 15TH

—1898	—1899—	1900---

SALARIES

$ 29,623.10	$31,817.65	$34,377.88

SUPPLIES, REPAIRS, Etc

" 2,059.53	" 2,717.01	" 2,595.54

SECRET SERVICE ACCOUNT

" 209.38	" 238.39	" 296.18

RENT OF POLICE ALARM

" 1,600.00	"1,600.00	"1,600.00

COST OF DEPARTMENT

$33,482.91	$36,375.05	$38,869.04

Total Fines, etc, Collected

$ 5,17761	$4,488.76	$6,555.20

Total Number of Arrests

3,438	3,681	4,414

Number of Days prison Confinement

14,833   13,365   15,698

Average daily Confinement

41   37   43

Total Cost Feeding Prisoners

$ 788.44 $ 803.04 $ 899.05

Average daily (Individual Cost)

$ .05 7-9 $ .06 $ .05 3-4

Days of Labor performed by Prisoners

5,764   6,409   7,160

Defective Bridges Reported

173   180   250

Defective Lights (out 3 hours)

1,872   740   505

Lost and Stolen Property Recovered

$ 2,726.00 $ 3,734.50 $ 4,864.95

Amount taken from and returned To Prisoners

$ 2,504.00 $ 2,158.00 $ 3,175.50

Number of Patrol Wagon Calls

1,607   1,569   1,984

Amount of Cash returned to Secret Service Account

$ 92.76 $ 95.44 $ 62.30

Showing the Following Improvements Over Last Year as Follows

Increase in Collections	$ 2,052.35
Increase in Labor performed	751 days
Increase in Number of Arrests	733
Increase in Stolen property recovered	$ 1,130.45
Decrease in Running Expenses	$ 121.47

EXHIBIT "A"

SHOWING AMOUNT OF FINES, BICYCLE LICENSES, AND INCIDENTAL COLLECTIONS PAID OVER TO THE CITY CLERK DURING THE YEAR ENDING MARCH 18TH-1900.

1899	FINES	SACKS, MANURE & HORSE FEED	FEEDING U.S. PRISONERS	BICYCLE TAGS	SALE HORSE
Mch 15-31	$ 118.00	$1.45		$1.50	
April	$ 284.00	$ .75		$8.50	
May	$ 370.00			$8.00	
June	$ 546.50	$3.65		$7.00	
July	$ 692.75	$ .25		$8.00	
August	$ 621.50	$ .55		$2.00	
September	$ 562.50	$ .80		$6.00	
October	$ 447.50	$1.65			
November	$ 574.50	$3.65			
December	$ 722.00	$4.90			$25.00
1900					
January	$ 569.80	$5.60	$9.90		
February	$540.50	$ .40			
March	$360.00	$8.00			$17.50
	$6,410.05	$31.65	$9.90		$58.50

Total Cash Collections………..$6,535.10

EXHIBIT "D"

SHOWING COST OF FEEDING PRISONERS FOR FISCAL YEAR
ENDING MARCH 15TH-1900

	PRISONERS FOR MONTH	DAILY AVERAGE OF PRISONERS	SUPPLIES FOR MONTH	DAILY AVERAGE OF SUPPLIES	INDIVIDUAL DAILY COST
1899 15TH to 31st. March....	558	37	$26.26	$ 1.75	.04—3/5
April....	1026	34	$59.30	$ 1.99	.05—4/5
May.....	1058	34	$61.54	$ 1.98	.05—4/5
June...	1315	45	$69.70	$ 2.32	.05—1/4
July...	1956	63	$112.80	$ 3.63	.05—3/4
August .	1528	48	$74.62	$ 2.40	.04—7/9
September.	1513	49	$89.93	$ 2.99	.05—8/10
October.	809	26	$48.38	$ 1.55	.06
November.	864	27	$51.80	$ 1.72	.06
December	1703	54	$94.08	$ 3.03	.05—1/2
1900 January.	1359	43	$80.76	$ 2.60	.05—1/5
February.	1303	46	$81.99	$ 2.92	.06—2/7
March.	706	47	$47.88	$ 3.19	.06—4/5
	15,698	43	$899.06	$ 2.46	.05—3/4

Daily Average of Prisoners Confined...........................46
Daily Average Cost of Supplies for Same.................$ 2.46
Daily Average Cost of Feeding Individual Prisoner..$.05—3/4

1899 Partial Annual Report

The 1899 report has not been found, but two portions of it were located on microfilm. They describe the inventory of the Patrol House and list a portion of the arrests made during the previous fiscal year which ended March 15, 1899.

EXHIBIT "H"
STOCK AND SUPPLIES IN PATROL HOUSE FOR YEAR
ENDING MARCH 15, 1899

VALUE

1	Patrol Wagon	$ 50.00
7	Horses	$ 775.00
1	Set Double Harness	$ 25.00
1	" Single Wagon Harness	$ 20.00
4	Patent Collars	$ 40.00
1	Pair Single Shafts	$ 5.00
8	Bridles	$ 9.00
7	Halters	$ 6.00
1	Curry Comb & Brush	$ .50
1	Mane Brush	$ .25
1	Feed Bin	$ 2.00
1	Feed Sifting Measure	$ .50
1	Wheel Barrow	$ 2.00
1	Rake & Shovel	$ 1.00
50	Feet Sprinkling Hose	$ 2.00
1	Lot Iron Pipe & Junk	$ 2.50
2	Pair Hand Cuffs	$ 7.00
1	" Wagon Lamps	$ 3.00
1	Stretcher For Wagon	$ 5.00
2	Horse Collars	$ 5.50
1	Saddles	$ 15.00
1	Rivet Punch & Set	$ 2.00
31	Window Sashes	$ 2.50
3	Scythe Blades & Handles	$ 5.00
1	Cupboard	$ 2.00
1	Heating Stove	$ 6.00

Amount Brought Forward $ 992.75

-C-I-T-Y V-I-O-L-A-T-I-O-N-S- -1-

Disorderly Conduct	1066
Dangerous & Supicious [sic]	905
Drunk	324

63

Drunk & Disorderly	221
Gaming	215
Safe Keeping	5
Contempt of Court	5
Doing Business Without License	66
Committing Nuisance	12
Bicycle Ordinance	48
Resisting Officer	45
Violation Quarantine Ordinance	3
Keeping Hogs in Pen	2
Discharging Fire Arms	14
Fugitive From Justice	6
Building Without Permit	3
Violation Vehicle Ordinance	159
Keeping Open Store On Sunday	14
Indecent Exposure	5
Violation Cab Ordinance	1
Jumping On Moving Street Cars	18
Discharging Fire Crackers	5
Violation Health Ordinance	59
Violation Sidewalk Ordinance	6
Violation Market Ordinance	6
Violation Prohibiting Escape	21
Jumping On Moving Trains	21
Violation Sanitary Ordinance	14
Furious Driving	3
Amount Brought Forward	3,272

Known Mobile Police Department Badges

The Mobile Police Department has had several badges throughout its history. There have been several versions of our Department badges that are not included in the following photographs. The badges shown and recognized are the badges that were issued to officers on the Department as the symbol of their authority granted to them as officers of the law.

Some of the variants include "detective," "traffic officer," "community resource," "jail," and special badges commissioned by a few of the chiefs. Chief Talley Rollings had a Chief's badge made with his name on it. That badge is currently displayed at Precinct Four. On June 18, 1867, Chief Dimon paid J. Howe $17.50 for the creation of seven silver badges. It is unknown what these badges looked like or to whom they were issued. In 1870, the City created a Secret Service Police Force, which is discussed in another chapter. That force had their own badge issued.

In 1867, during reconstruction, Chief Dimon and the Mayor utilized men in an undercover operation to spy on citizens and current members of the Police Department. These spies reported on the activities and suspected "rebellious" leanings of individuals, which lead to the dismissal of several individuals from positions on the department or with the city. It is possible these badges ordered by Dimon were for their use, though it is equally plausible that they were created for him and his assistant chiefs.

1. **Number 36 Badge**

   Pre 1860s to 1865, possibly used until 1872

2. **Circle Star Badge**

   1872 to 1890s

3. **Circle Star Badge with filigree**

   1890s to 1913

4. **Breast Shield Badge**

   1913 to 1950

5. **Breast Shield Badge with Eagle**

   1950 to 1962

6. **Six Flags Badge with Patrolman**

   1962-1980s

7. **Six Flags Badge with Police Officer**

   1980s to 2023

8. **Six Flags Badge Tricentennial**

   2002 (approved for wear during the year)

9. **Six Flags Badge with Stars and Bars**

   2023-current

   (The stars and bars replaced the battle flag)

Number 36 Badge (replica is number 37)
Pre-1860s to 1865, maybe in use until 1872

History of Badge 36

The collector who currently has possession of badge #36, purchased the badge from another relic hunter many years ago. The collector said the relic hunter related to him that he had found the badge in 1965 while metal detecting at the scene of the Battle of Spanish Fort, which occurred from March 27 to April 9, 1865.

The battle of Spanish Fort/Fort Blakely was the last major battle of the Civil War. The Fort Blakely portion of this battle occurred six hours after General Robert E. Lee surrendered the Army of Northern Virginia to General Ulysess S. Grant at the Appomattox Court House on April 9, 1865. There were an estimated seven hundred forty-four Confederate casualties during this battle with an estimated two hundred fifty killed in action. The City of Mobile surrendered to Union forces on April 12, 1865.

We have documentation that several Mobile Police Officers joined the Confederate Army, and several were members of the 1st Regiment, Mobile Volunteers that were also known as Mobile Guards or Mobile Regiment. This could explain how the badge ended up at the site of a battle.

Major Wilbur Williams was able to photograph the badge, and Symbol Arts Company was able to make one hundred replicas. The badge made by Symbol Arts Company is identical to the original found badge in all regards, other than the number. The original is number 36 and the replica is number 37. These badges were sold on a first-come basis eighty-six of them were purchased by various officers, both active and retired. The remaining fourteen were donated to the Mobile Optimist Club and were presented to Officer of the Month recipients. Synovus Bank has purchased additional badges, and they have provided these badges to recipients of Officer of the Month for several years.

This is the only known example of the oldest recognized MPD badge in existence. Major Wilbur Williams has extensively studied and researched this topic, and it is his belief that this is also the oldest known law enforcement badge from any agency in Alabama and most probably the entire southern part of the country as Mobile Police Department is the oldest established police department in the state.

We cannot establish the exact dates of this badge, but based on known information, we can establish the following positions.

1. We know that the seal depicted on the badge was the seal of the State of Alabama, known as the "map and tree" which was used until it was changed in 1868.

2. If the badge was discovered buried at the site of the Battle of Spanish Fort, it would have been made prior to the battle, May 27-April 8, 1865.

3. Experts believe the design, craftsmanship, and material used dates to late 1850s or early 1860s.

4. It is believed and probable that the badge was ordered sometime in 1858 at the direction of the new Chief of Police, Stephen David Charpentier. He had ordered new uniforms as well, and it is believed that the badges were ordered at the same time. That fits with the historian's belief that the craftsmanship dates to late 1850s to early 1860s.

Additionally, we know that on February 12, 1872, the Council approved the request of the Department to purchase one hundred new "circle star" badges that were sequentially numbered from one to one hundred. The approved expenditure for these badges was $100. There is no record of what company made the badges.

Circle Star Badge, 1872

Circle Star Badge with Filigree Pattern, 1890s

**Breast Shield along with Eagle over top on
Hat Shield, 1913**

Breast Shield with Eagle, 1950-1962 (approximate)
Photographs show that this badge was used as early
as 1948 in conjunction with the earlier version badge.
Both styles were captured in photographs of older officers
with newer officers.

Six Flags Badge with "Patrolman," 1962

**Six Flags Badge and Hat Shield
with "Police Officer," 1980s**

Six Flags Tricentennial Badge 2002

Six Flags Badge with Stars and Bars, 2023-now

McShane Bell

The bell that is currently displayed in front of Police Headquarters at 2460 Government Boulevard has a long history of service to the City of Mobile. The bell was ordered by the City of Mobile and manufactured by McShane Bell Foundry in Baltimore, Maryland, in 1881. We know that it arrived via rail car, and it was placed in the Old Guard House at 29 Conti Street, near St. Emanuel Street.

According to Caldwell Delaney's *A History of Mobile,* the Old Guard House was occupied from about 1839 to about 1896, and it had a watch tower and a bell.

In 1896, a new Mobile Police Building was constructed at 57 St. Emanuel Street between Conti and Government Streets. It is believed that the bell was placed in the steeple of this building during construction. Photographs show the bell in the steeple. Documents from 1902 indicate that the bell was placed at police headquarters and was used as a fire alarm. The Police Building at this location remained occupied until 1950, when a new police building was built at 51 Government Street.

When the police vacated the building on St. Emanuel Street and occupied the new Police Building on April 17, 1950, the bell came with them. It was placed in front of the building, reportedly at the request of the then Police Chief, Dudley McFadyen (1941-1961). The bell's yoke and clapper have been lost.

In January 1991, the current Police Headquarters was purchased and occupied. The bell was transferred to its current location at that time.

While planning for the construction of a new Headquarters building in 2018 to present, I felt that it was important to plan for the display of the bell. I discovered that McShane Bell Foundry had been sold, and the Baltimore foundry closed. The McShane Bell Foundry is now located in Maryland Heights, Missouri. I contacted the vice president of the company, William Parker, and he advised that the company could refurbish our bell.

On June 18, 2021, I received an estimate for the refurbishment, including a new yoke, clapper, and swinging wheel in the amount of $6,750. Freight would run about $800.

Below is a photograph of the bell from a Mobile Register article dated June 27, 1965.

The bell in its current location, 2460 Government Blvd.

The inscription on the bell:

MC SHANE BELL FOUNDRY
HENRY MC SHANE & CO.
BALTIMORE, MD.
1881.

Headquarters Buildings

The original city prison/jail was located in the old Fort Conde/Charlotte complex. It was described as being very old and barbaric. In 1824, the U.S. Government donated an "L" shaped piece of property between Royal Street and St. Emanuel Street, with a frontage on Conti Street and a smaller frontage on St. Emanuel Street, to the City of Mobile. That was the location to be used for a new jail.

On April 8, 1829, the new Police Station and City Prison were completed at 29 Conti Street. That facility remained in use until a fire on October 7-8, 1839, erupted in Mobile that destroyed over five hundred buildings, including the Police Station and City Prison. Efforts to rebuild were immediately made.

The Old Guard House 1829-1896

On June 15, 1841, the new Guard House and City Prison were completed at a cost of $6,392. It was upgraded in 1843 by the addition of brick walls, nine inches thick, to the front of the building on Conti Street and an additional wall added to the west side of the building that faced St. Emanuel Street. Iron spikes were added to the top of the ten-foot wall at three-inch intervals. The Old Guard House was the police headquarters, jail, mayor's office, armory, Mayor's Court, fire watch station, and Fire Station for Engine Company 2. It remained in use until a new Police Headquarters was built in 1896.

Police Headquarters at 57 St. Emanuel Street 1896-1950

Police Headquarters 51 Government Street,
1950-1990

Police Headquarters, 2460 Government Blvd.
1990-Present.

John Henry Bressingham
The longest serving officer in MPD history

John H. Bressingham was born October 25, 1866. He resided at 403 S. Jefferson Street. A document from the early 1900s indicates that he was hired on April 29, 1894, but there is documentation that he was employed as a "special officer" in 1890. He worked until early 1944 when his health deteriorated due to his injury from being shot in 1901 and the accumulation of injuries sustained in his lengthy career. The City kept Officer Bressingham on the Police Department pay roll at full pay until his death on May 29, 1950. He is buried in Magnolia Cemetery, Square 27, Lot 102 with his wife, Mary.

Census notes from 1870 indicate that his parents were Jas. Bressingham, 45 years of age, from Ireland and Johanna Bressingham, 40 years of age. This census lists John as 3 years of age and a sister, Mary, as 5 years of age. The census also lists a John Bressingham, 40 years of age, from Ireland, currently employed as a policeman. John was married to Kate Bressingham, 25 years of age, from Ireland. It is believed that this John was John Henry's uncle. He was on the payroll of the police department for some years, and in the 1869 City Directory, John Bressingham is identified as the assistant chief. After that year, he was on the rolls as a policeman.

John H. Bressingham is found on the police payroll in 1891 as a "special officer." On April 29, 1894, he was hired as a full-time police officer. It is known that he drove the horse-drawn wagon for some time.

Day shift payroll sheet from December 22, 1893,
listing Bressingham as a Special.

Photograph of Bressingham from the 1890s

On Sunday, March 31, 1901, he was working with Detective Edward Morris and Officer Edward McGrath attempting to capture two escaped convicts from the Jennings and Brother turpentine camp of Manistee, Alabama, near Monroeville. William Davis and William Kilpatrick, two Black men, had escaped the camp with another Black man, and on December 19, 1900, they killed the Marshall of Gulfport, Mississippi. One of the suspects was captured in Gulfport and lynched. A report came in that the remaining two convicts were now in Mobile.

A "Daily Register" newspaper article dated Tuesday, April 2, 1901, states that on Sunday, March 31, 1901, Detective Morris and Officers Bressingham and McGrath were in plain clothes, in the hopes of not startling the suspects. They found the escaped men at the Mobile, Jackson and Kansas City railroad depot, located at Tennessee Street and Conception Street. The three approached the convicts when Morris asked what time the next train was leaving. As Morris attempted to arrest Davis, a struggle ensued where Davis produced a pistol and fired. The first round fired by Davis penetrated Morris' left shoulder, exited, and entered Bressingham's right side, penetrating his lung. The fight was hand-to-hand, with gunfire erupting for about ten minutes with a total of fifteen shots fired. Officer Bressingham emptied his revolver, attempted to load again but the second round jammed. He removed the round, closed the cylinder, and shot Davis, who was still fighting Morris, in the head. Davis fought for a few moments longer and then slumped to the ground. Kilpatrick had fled the scene on foot and the three officers jumped in a coach and returned to the Police Building, where Chief Soost met them. Morris and Bressingham were gravely wounded, and a physician was called. Officer Morris was shot four times, once in the shoulder, once in the left jawbone, emerging through the right cheek, once in the hip and once in the lower abdomen. This is the wound that would ultimately prove fatal. Bressingham was shot in the right side, with the bullet entering his lung. Both officers were taken to their homes. A search party was able to locate Kilpatrick near Fulton Street and Government Street to the west of the city.

On Monday, April 1, 1901, at 8:30 pm, Detective Morris passed away at his home at 27 Spring Hill Shell Road.

Officer Bressingham fought through his wound and fever and made a recovery. He was healed enough to return to duty, but his injury would plague him for the rest of his life.

Several newspaper articles were written about Officer Bressingham over the years. He worked at the Old Guard House on Conti Street, the new Police Building on St. Emanuel Street, and was alive to see the new police building being constructed on Government Street.

Below are letters written about Officer Bressingham and his physical condition. They will be attached, and they are interesting in the fact that the Department and the City held Officer Bressingham in such high regard and he was so well-respected for his service that they fought to pay him for life.

On July 3, 1940, Chief of Police, E.V. Warren wrote a letter to Police Commissioner Cecil Bates requesting authorized sick leave for Officer Bressingham.

On November 29, 1940, Chief Warren sent a letter to the Mayor, Cecil Bates, requesting a thirty-day leave of absence for Officer Bressingham due to illness. Mayor Cecil Bates forwarded this with an additional letter to the Director of Personnel, Harry Pillans.

On February 2, 1944, Mayor Robin Herndon sent a letter to the Director of Personnel Harry Pillans, stating that Officer Bressingham was unable to resume his full duties, and in the public interest, they should pay him his full salary until his death. They felt he was entitled to this full consideration due to the severe injuries he received at the time of Detective Morris' death.

On February 10, 1944, Personnel Director Pillans sent a letter to the Board of City Commissioners indicating the approval of paying Officer Bressingham half-pay for life.

On February 11, 1944, Director Pillans sent another letter, apologizing for his mistake. Officer Bressingham would be paid FULL PAY for life.

84

The Police Department Payroll and Employee Record book from 1944 indicates John Bressingham received a salary of $110 each month that year. I can find no documentation if this was what his full salary was but compared to other officers of the same rank that year, he was paid $50 less each month.

Officer Bressingham passed away in 1950.

1932 Police inspection in front of the Police Building.
Bressingham is standing, 2nd from left.

The First Black Officers in Mobile

There is always curiosity about firsts. Being first in anything has its rewards, such as pride, satisfaction in a job well done, or being first in paving a way for others to follow. In Mobile, we recognize W.O. Powell and Walter Jackson as being the first black police officers on the MPD. That is certainly true in the "modern era," but a study of documents from the late 1860s shows that during the Reconstruction era in Mobile, there were several black officers hired, and one was promoted to assistant chief.

Some of these documents are housed at the University of Alabama Special Collections Library. In November 2024, I was able to obtain digital copies of the collection. The collection contains several thousand pages of Police Department communications, applications, letters, etc., dated from 1865-1869. After the Civil War ended, and after the appointment of General Pope as the military commander during Reconstruction, political leaders and police officers alike were dismissed from service. Others were appointed and political changes enacted. General Pope dismissed Charpentier as police chief and appointed Colonel C.A.R. Dimon as chief.

Under Chief Dimon and Mayor Horton's leadership in 1867, there were thirty-three black men hired as police officers. The first five were hired on July 1, 1867. As recorded in the book *Down the Years*, pg. 175, and in a written order from Chief Dimon, these first five were Allen Alexander, John Barber, Felix Robinson, D.C. Thompson, and John Tobin. In Chief Dimon's order issued that day, he also dismissed a lieutenant, a sergeant, and six privates (officers) from the Department. In August of that year, Ovide Gregory was promoted from Lieutenant of the Watch to one of the four assistant chief positions. Ovide was a Creole leader and had been prominent in Mobile since before the Civil War. He was a member of the Alabama Constitutional Convention and legislature.

The political divisions continued to grow and throughout the reconstruction period, the city was quite divided. I can find no record of when Assistant Chief Ovide Gregory and the other black men were no longer on the rolls. Until the early 1900s with the adoption of civil service positions and protections under the Personnel Board, officers were often dismissed for minor infractions or when a new chief or mayor took office.

A newspaper article dated January 22, 1954, states that the City Commission hired William O. Powell and Walter P. Jackson as police officers with a start date of February 1, 1954. They are the first black men hired in the modern era of the Police Department, and they are recognized as the first black men to wear a badge in the State of Alabama. William Powell worked in the Department for a few years and then departed for civilian employment. Mr. Powell is buried in Andalusia, Alabama.

Corporal Walter Jackson

Walter Jackson retired from the Department on May 17, 1994. He passed away on December 22, 2005. The First

Precinct at Virginia Street and Broad Street was named after Walter Jackson.

On the Mobile Police Department website in March 2000, a section was dedicated to the black officers of the Mobile Police Department. The section stated the following:

Mr. William O. Powell and Mr. Walter P. Jackson were both hired on February 1, 1954. Both Powell and Jackson were born in Mobile. Mr. Powell had attended Talladega College and was employed at a local shipyard when he learned of the openings in the police department. Mr. Powell openly admits he applied as somewhat of a challenge, just to see if a black man could obtain a position as a police officer in Mobile, Alabama.

On the other hand, Mr. Jackson had a long-standing, close relationship with the police department since his grandfather was employed as a porter with the Department. As a result, Mr. Jackson had been around for years and was known and respected by many of the high-ranking officers on the Department.

Tyree Richburg was hired on August 1, 1954, and he became the first black officer promoted to sergeant. He retired as a lieutenant in 1978. He became the U.S. Marshal for the Southern District of Alabama and then acted as Chief of Police in Prichard, Alabama, until 1983.

Harold Johnson was hired in 1990 to be the Chief of Police and retired in 1996.

Chief Johnson's story will be on forthcoming pages. (See the 1990s section.)

1850s

Annual Report by the City Marshal
December 1, 1856

The following text is taken from the Annual Report of the City Marshal December 1, 1856, it is reproduced as written. There are some interesting points made, and this document, I believe, set the City of Mobile on the path to creating a more efficient, uniformed department that was led by a Police Chief. Following the report by City Marshal Maury is a recommendation for changes in the force by Mayor J M Withers dated December 29, 1856, and an amendment to those recommendations by the City Aldermen adopted on January 2, 1857.

There were suggestions for regulations and ordinances to be written that defined the duties and responsibilities of the officers included in the original letters, but those have not been located. Marshal Maury also made a request for badges and hats to distinguish officers from citizens. There is no documented response to those requests, but as stated in another chapter of this history, badges were obtained in 1858-1860 by Chief of Police Stephen Charpentier. It is clear that City Marshal Harry Maury was a dedicated leader of the Department, and he was aware of the changes that needed to be made to improve the professionalism and efficiency of the Mobile Police Department. He served as City Marshal on two occasions, the last was from January 9, 1856, to January 22, 1858.

To the Mayor, Aldermen, and Common Council of the City of Mobile.
Gentlemen:
I deem it my duty to make to your honorable body a breif [sic] statement of the operations of the Police under my charge for the past year, and respectfully to suggest such changes as I

believe would improve the efficiency of the Departarment [sic].

The Police of the City for the greater part of the past year has been composed of fifty men all told. Besides myself, we have had three deputy Marshals elected by the Mayor, Aldermen, & Common Council; one Captain, one Lieutenant, four Sergeants, and forty night watchmen appointed by the Mayor; the total expense of which is about $24,768 - dollars. Since the 1st of December 1855 the Police Department has paid into the City treasury about $16,474 – dollars.

The number of arrests during that time has been four thousand eight hundred and thirty two; (4,832) of which two thousand six hundred and thirty (2,630) have been made exclusively by the day police, consisting of four men, all told.

From this you will readily perceive the great disproportion existing between the day and the night police in point of members and service required.

The duties of the day officers are extremely arduous, & their salaries small. The Deputy Marshals, three in number, besides being looked to exclusively for detective business, have to see to the quietness of the City throughout the day and often until a late hour at night. In addition to the pulling and hauling of drunken men and women from all parts of the City, it is their duty to see that all sidewalks are kept in good repair and unobstructed; to see to the licenses of all hotels, boarding houses, barrooms, cabs, drays, shows &c. &c.; to subpoena witnesses, execute warrant, watch and catch thieves, watch the arrival and departure of all boats and trains of cars, and do suchlike duties as may be required of them by the Mayor or the Marshal. The interests of the City demand ceaseless vigilance on the part of these officers, and, to insure [sic] this, their pay should place them above the necessity of looking for work outside their regular official duties.

And here I may be excused for reminding your honorable bodies of the successful manner in which these duties have been performed by the officers associated with me during the last year. Not a professional theif [sic] been here but he has been detected & either brought to justice or sent from the City. Almost every theft or burglary has been traced to the parties committing it & the property recovered; evil-doers & fugitives from justice abroad have here been promptly arrested & sent back for trial; fires have been unusually rare, and out City is a model of tranquility and order. The serious evil of trafficking with slaves, although not entirely eradicated, has received its death blow, and slave owners bear cheerful testimony of the improvement in their negroes.

Appended to this report will be found a minute statemen of the matter and causes of arrest during the year. *(this document cannot be located)*

By far the most unsatisfactory and imperfect part of this Department is the present system of the night-watch. The privates are paid (or rather promised,) thirty-five dollars per month, and are divided into two watches, each of which is on duty only half the night; there being, of course, never more than twenty men on duty at one time. From the smallness of the pay and other causes, the post of night-watchman is only sought as a last resort either by those who are so unfortunate as not to be able to obtain other employment, or by those who are too indolent or too worthless for anything else. The best of our watchmen are obliged to seek employment during the day or eke out their scanty pittance for the support of their families, and as soon as more lucrative business is obtained, they quit the Police to make room for some other unfortunate and inexperienced applicant. The consequence is that we have continually for City guardians an entire set of strangers; men who scarcely know the streets of the City, and who cannot distinguish the most notorious thieves from respectable Citizens.

To remedy this evil, I respectfully recommend that the number of the night watch be diminished to thirty men; that their pay be increased, and that they be required to do eight hours of duty instead of four.

The effect of this would be, I think, to give us a steady & permanent set of watchmen, who would seek no other employment. They would consider the increase of pay an ample compensation for the extra service, and by looking upon the police as their profession, they would in a short time know and be known to all of our Citizens- which would add greatly to their fitness and efficiency.

I would also suggest the necessity of distinguishing the night watchmen from other Citizens by some uniform badge of office. Being men who are not selected on account of any particular shrewdness in police matters, no <u>detective</u> business is required of them, and there is no reason why they should be unknown. Their business is the <u>prevention</u> of crime and disorder; to assist citizens and strangers in cases of need; and to maintain order and quiet in the City during the night. The very presence of an officer, if known, will frequently prevent serious affrays; whereas the abrupt interference of a stranger, not known as a policeman, and flourishing a big stick, serves only to increase the difficulty, and our watchmen are sometimes very roughly handled by evil-doers under the excuse that "they did not recognize them as officers-" Stranders, also, coming to our City are often in want of an officer and are unable to find one; they are frequently imposed on by men falsely representing themselves as officers. Many of our own citizens are under the impression that they traverse half the City at night without once meeting a watchman, simply because they cannot, under the present system, distinguish a watchman from anyone else.

My proposition is to supply each night watchman with a hat similar to those worn by members of fire companies, on the front of which shall appear, in plain letters, "City Guard, No.-" Our streets patrolled by steady, respectable watchmen thus equipped, I am satisfied we should have less trouble, and our citizens would feel more confident by being well guarded.

In view of the constant difficulties arising from the total absence of any Police Regulations, or any ordinances defining the powers and duties of the Police officers, I herewith respectfully submit to your honble [sic] bodies, for your approval, a system of Police, drawn up with great care and after much study; setting forth, in addition to General Rules, the powers & duties of every officer and employe [sic] in the Police Departt [sic], and I earnestly ask that, should this system not meet your approbation, the police Committee may be instructed to adopt & substitute, as it is impossible for this Department to be advantageously organized under the present loose discipline and entire absence of system.

*(missing text)*s to these Regulations, I have drawn them up without regard to the present incumbents in office, and solely with a view to increase the efficiency of the Police Department of the City of Mobile, the reorganization of which has been for the past year my duty and my pride.

93

Very Respectfully,

Your obt servant

Harry Maury

City Marshal.

Endorsements:

No 1 Annual Report from H Maury Marshal

Refd (with regulations) *(proposed regulations have not been located)*
To Joint Police Comte (sic)
    Dec. 11, 1856

_____

Concur'd in by C C
12 Decemr. 56.

RECOMMENDED FEW CHANGES IN CITY'S FORCE
Dec. 29, 1856

                                    Mayors Office
                                    City of Mobile,
Dec 29th 1856

To the Boards of Aldermen & Common Council

With the termination of the Municipal Year, expired, the term for which the various Officers of the City were elected, and since that period the Official Boards required, have been null & void at least as to the Securities.

The Charter requires that the Watch to guard & protect the City shall be appointed by the Mayor, the number only to be designated by the Boards. This duty was performed by you at an early period of the past Municipal year, the Charter not specifying how often or at what time it shall be done. No change having been provided for by the Boards for the present year, and not deeming myself any change in numbers or designations advisable, I shall for the protection of the Community from the unrestrained lawlessness continue the City Guard as constituted the past year. The only change which I deem it my duty to recommend, is as the renumeration of the Guard- The following I believe would conduce to the public interest

> For Capt. Guard, at the rate of $1000 pr annum
> "   Lieut "   " "   "   " $ 800 "   "

For the 4 Sergeants, each- $50   per month
"   "   40 private watch, $45   "   "   each
"   "   1 Day and 1 night Sentinel, each, $60. pr month
"   "   3 Bell Sentinels, each, ------------$60   "   "

Any change from the present system, requiring longer & continuous service from the Police, would in my judgment but impair its activity, force out the best men from the Service and end in demoralization.

J M Withers

Endorsements:

Communication from the Mayor

Communication recd & enclosed resolution adopted by C C Dec 29. 1856

The Aldn concur as amended within Jany 2. 1857

The Council concur in the Amendments of Aldn

Amendment of Aldermen—adopted Jay 2/57

Amend by striking out $1000 and inserting $800 as salry
[sic]
    for Capt of Guard

Strike out $800 and insert $600 for Lieut –

and strike out 40 watch at $45 & insert
25 watch at $55 pr mo.

                    Concurred in by C C 2 Jany 57

RESOLUTION ADOPTED
Dec 29, 1856

(adopted by C C – 29 Decr. [sic] 56)

(In pencil)

Resolved

That the Boards of Aldermen & Common Council
approve of the appointments of one Captain, of the
Guard one Lieut of the Guard,, four Sergeants of the
Guard and Forty Privates one day and one night Sentinel & Three Bell sentinels – at the Salaries ex-
pressed in the communication of His Honor the Mayor
dated 29th Decr= & addressed to the Boards of Alder-

men & Common Council –

Endorsements:

Resolution by Councilman
Woodruff – on giving the
Mayor Officers & Guards.

_____

Adopted by C C
29 Decem. 56.

Jany 2d Concurred
in as amended
within

Jany 2d. The Council
concur in Aldns
action

_____

1860s

Police Chief Stephen Charpentier returned to Mobile in 1865 from commanding a light artillery company in the Confederate Army and resumed his previous position as Chief. As noted in another chapter, Stephen Charpentier was the first person to lead the Mobile Police Department as Chief of Police. Charpentier had previously been an Assistant Marshal until 1858 when he was named City Marshal. Around that same time the City of Mobile changed the title to Chief of Police, so Charpentier became the first official Chief of Police of the Mobile City Police Department.

Upon returning, Charpentier wanted to improve the image of the police officers, so he decided to order new uniforms. Charpentier consulted local merchants and eventually new police uniforms were ordered from a firm in New York City, and the design of the new uniforms were identical in all respects, including color, to the Central Park Police of New York. Today we call them the NYPD. Around the time the uniforms were received, Congress instituted Military Reconstruction for the City of Mobile on May 2, 1867. All elected officials were notified that their positions were provisional.

Mayor Withers had communicated with the Commanding General regarding the police uniforms, but on May 14, 1867, Mayor Withers wrote to the members of the Board of Aldermen and the Common Council.

Gentlemen of the Board of Aldermen and Common Council,

The Communication of the 24th ult, from the General Commanding the "District of Alabama" transmitted herewith, will sufficiently explain why the City Police have not been required to wear the Uniforms prescribed and furnished by the City. The fact of its being identical with that worn by the Central Park Police the City of New York and that no political significance was intended, or should be attached to the color of the cloth, was communicated to the Gen. Comdg.

I recommend that you require the uniforms to be returned to the Chief of Police for safe keeping and proper preservation; and that the Treasurer be instructed to refund to each policeman the amount paid by him.

J. W. Withers

Chief of Police Dimon

On May 22, 1867, Major General John Pope ordered the removal of Mayor Jones M. Withers as Mayor and Stephen Charpentier as Chief of Police. Major General Pope ordered the appointment of Colonel Charles Augusta Ropes Dimon as Chief of Police. Dimon had served in the Union Army since the beginning of the war and eventually retired as Brigadier General after his service as Chief of Police in Mobile. Dimon returned to his home state of Massachusetts and eventually served as Mayor of Lowell, Massachusetts.

The new uniforms remained stored until March 1868, when Chief Dimon revisited the issue with the Board of Aldermen and Common Council.

March 11, 1868
Office of Chief of Police
Mobile, Ala. Mch 11th 1868

To the Honorable Boards of Aldermen and Common Council

Gentlemen:

I have had the Honor to call your attention on some three different occasions to the fact of there now remaining on hand the property of the City some one

hundred and twenty-five Gray Uniforms for the Police Force which have been ordered and paid for. An order from Gen. Pope, Comig. 3rd Military Dist, prohibited the wearing of them and I now request authority to make some disposition of them for the best interest of the City.
Very Respectfully
Your Obt. Svt.
C. A. R. Dimon
Chief of Police

Shortly after this letter was written, Chief Dimon ordered the police uniforms burned during a public gathering in Bienville Square.

1868

The following is a portion of the annual report submitted by Chief Dimon on January 1, 1868. It is recorded as written. The complete report has not been found. Following it is a report from Sam J. Magill, Captain of the Watch to the Chief of Police that describes the staffing and pay scale for the Department from 1850 to 1868. These documents are a part of the collection housed at the University of Alabama Special Collections Library.

Office of Chief of Police
Mobile, Alabama,
January 1" 1868
To Hon. G. Horton- Mayor.
And Honorable Board of Alderman & Common ?

Gentlemen-
I have the honor to submit the following report of the operations of the Police Department, of this city, from the 22" day of May, 1867, to the 31st day of December, 1867, inclusive. Attached to the report are schedules, lettered from A to ?,

showing the organization of the force at the present time, the total number of arrests, a synopsis of the crimes for which the arrests were made, operations of the sanitary police, changes ? taking charge, amount of finances received, account of fines received, account of disposition of "Secret Service Fund" and Record of deaths.

Schedule A.

Shows the organization of the force and the number of members at the present time.

The changes since the commencement of my tour of duty have been various, occasioned by discharges for neglect of duty, without cause, resignation, appointments and deaths.

The duties of the chief for the last six months have been extremely arduous, in consequence to the many changes in the reorganization and disciplining of the force. The Assistant Chiefs are on duty during the day, one acting officer of the day at police station from 11 o'clock a.m., until 8 o'clock pm: the day police are on duty for the same length of time. The captain of watch, lieutenants and night patrol report for duty at 8 p.m. and are relieved at 6 a.m., this will be changed as the season advances and the nights grow shorter.

Schedule B,

Exhibits the total number of arrests, of prosecutions, and of persons arrested and discharged without prosecution. How these statistics compare with those of previous years, I am unable to state as no record can be found of any prior reports having been made. This shows but a small portion of the work which as been done as their (sic) are a great many cases on record of complaints, where it was not ? necessary to issue warrants or make arrests, from various cases, cases are constantly arising and brought before the officers for adjustment, the disposition of which, requires quick perception, good discrimination and sound judgement.

Schedule C, shows the offences for which the arrests were made, the number of arrests, and the number of each offense. The excessive use of intoxicating liquors, is the principal cause of the crimes brought before the court. The large number of persons arrested during the last eight months for drunkenness, disorderly conduct, petty larceny, and crimes of a minor nature directs attention to the necessity of some provision being made for additional punishment than that of short imprisonment and it is to be regretted that Major General Swayne, commanding the District of Alabama, deemed it necessary to issue an order abolishing the "chain gang" and I respectfully recommend, that some action be taken in the matter by your honor and honorable board.

In the schedule of deaths all have been occasioned by the prevailing epidemic of last summer, and in the greater number of these cases with ? were exposed.

Schedule D. exhibits the total amount of fines imposed and the amount which has been received within the last eight months.

Schedule E shows the amount expended on account of the "Secret Service Fund", which expenditures has been actually necessary in the organization of this branch of the service, rendering the police force more efficient in preventing crime by the aid of a ? detective system.

The duties devolving upon the sanitary police, although of a disagreeable character, are of inestimable value to the inhabitants of the city and ? be properly appreciated by those who are aggravated with the daily experiences of those who have to discharge them.

The lack of an adequate system of drainage, connected with the fact that comparatively few of the streets of Mobile are paved and all deposits there are quickly absorbed thereby becoming part of the soil, which exposed to the rays of the sun, produce an exhalation that is both unpleasant to the smell and deleterious to health. These are matters which, I respectfully suggest are worthy of due consideration by the departments to which they properly belong.

The force has been increased within the last six months. Six (6) privates, A branch station, for the better protection of citizens living in the western portion of this city, has been located at the West Ward Hotel on the Springhill Road, with a permanent force consisting of, One (1) Sergeant two (2)

Corporals and eleven (11) privates whose duty it is to guard the city west of Broad Street.

I would respectfully recommend the adoption of what is known as the six (6) hour relief system, thereby diminishing one half the length of duty, increasing the discipline and efficiency of the force and improving the health of its members, and giving at all times in reserve at the Guard House which in the present politically excited state of the community, is much to be desired. The great number discharged for neglect of duty and other causes, involving much time and labor in disciplining new members, having more or less the effect of disenergizing [sic] the force, has been occasioned in my judgement, by improper selections, on account of the want of neutral and physical qualifications before appointment.

I would suggest in future, that all candidates be subjected to a thorough examination by city surgeon as to their physical ability to endure the fatigue and exposure, incident to a policeman's life and before entering upon their duties receive a certificate of general capacity signed, after examination, by the mayor and joint Police Committee.

By servicing this course, it is my opinion there will be placed upon the force a class of men of the best material and qualification that can be obtained and I am confident with proper officers the force will compare favorably with any police force in the country. I would, also, respectfully recommend that the power of appointment and removal be left entirely with the Mayor and his joint Police Committee. It is almost impossible to give any statistics of the workings of the detective officers of this force that would adequately represent the amount of service actually performed by these officers as the greater portion of their work makes no show on the records. They are often required to watch known thieves or suspected characters, for days and weeks results of which no computation can be made, patience, industry shrewdness and tact must be brought into constant exercise by the respectful detective officers and it is believed that the work ? of the detectives of this department has been well done and has given satisfaction to the public.

It is strongly recommended that the battery and apparatus connected with the fire alarm telegraph be removed to the Central Police Station, that all boxes connect directly with that station and the alarm repeated from that place to engine houses and other parts of the city. It is believed if this plan is adopted, fewer false alarms will occur and the parties tampering with boxes can be brought to justice.

I cannot think that the police force can decrease at present without great risk to the city. At least until after the coming elections are over.

I shall be able with my next report to ? my statistical information by giving nativity-occupation-"married or single" "can or cannot read or write" of every person committed to the Guard House for crime. And other valuable information which the labor and time attending the disciplining and reorganizing of the present force have prevented be from doing- the many necessary changes in the force are much to be respected and sufficient

Number of Police employed and amount of salary paid from 1850 to 1868

```
1850 to 1851 -  35  men  at  $35   pr Month
1852 to 1862    40   "    "  $40  "    "
1862  "  1865   50   "    "  $100 "    "
In       1865   60   "    "  $45  "    "
In       1866   75   "    "  $75  "    "
```

for the above amount of pay the men was on duty half the night

1867_____   75 men at $100 pr month for all night

The above was the strength of the night force and I am informed there was only about (6) or (8) men employed on the day force under the instruction of a Marshall or Superintendent of Police up to about 1858 when the first Chief was appointed.

Most Respectfully

Sam J. Magill
Capt Watch

To Chief Police

1870s

Secret Service Police

On July 8, 1870, the Board of Aldermen for the City of Mobile created an ordinance to establish a "secret police force." The motion was tabled until July 18, 1870, when it was adopted into law. The ordinance stated that the Mayor was granted the authority to organize a secret force from the existing numbers of the police force to be under his special supervision. The number of secret officers would not exceed seven men, and the newly created force was authorized to include a chief or superior officer. The new chief or superior officer and the men selected would be under the direction of the mayor, or in the mayor's absence, be subordinate to the Chief of Police.

This was a formal creation of an already existing entity in Mobile. When Reconstruction began in Mobile in early May 1867, Mayor Horton and Chief Dimon began utilizing and funding a group of "undercover or secret" men to spy on citizens and police officers. These spies would report any "rebellious" activities or political leanings that went against the newly military appointed civilian authority. Officers and other city employees were fired based on information provided by these spies. Documents show that these spies issued reports in secret and their written correspondence was not signed by name. As early as May 31, 1867, there is a bill from the Waverly Stables for the rental of horses and buggies that were paid for from the "Secret Service Fund".

On April 14, 1874, the ordinance was referred to the
Police Committee for review. The 1884 annual report from the
city indicates that the total expenditures for the Secret Service
the year preceding was $14.20. The last report I can find on
the Secret Service expenditures is in the 1912 annual report. It
states that the total was $830.90.

Police Bond, 1871

(Officers had to be bonded to work in the city.)

The State of Alabama, Mayor's Office.

CITY OF MOBILE.

We, _Thomas Barrett_ _____

_____

acknowledge ourselves to be in debt to the Mayor, Aldermen and Common Council of the City of Mobile, and their successors in Office, in the sum of _Five Hundred_ Dollars, for the payment of which, we bind ourselves, and our heirs, executors, administrators and assigns, jointly and severally by these presents.

Signed with our hands and seals this _1st_ day of _January_ 1871.

On condition, that whereas the said _Thomas Barrett_ was on the _1st_ day of _January_ A. D., 1871, appointed _a Private on The Police Force_ by the Mayor of the City of Mobile for the Municipal year ending the 31st day of December, 1871.

If he shall faithfully execute and perform the duties of his Office according to the provisions of the Charter of the City of Mobile, and the several amendments thereto, and all orders, ordinances, by-laws and resolutions of the Mayor, Aldermen and Common Council of the City of Mobile, now in force, or hereafter to be made, to the satisfaction of the said Mayor, Aldermen, and Common Council, then this obligation to be null and void, otherwise to remain in full force and effect.

Witness:

Thomas Barrett (LS)

James McDonald (LS)

Michael Davis (LS)

(LS)

Approved
Jany 21/71
M Horst
Mayor

Felix McCulloch Secretary

1872

The year 1872 was a very interesting and eventful year for the Mobile Police Department. On Monday, January 3, 1872, William P. Barlow became Chief of Police. The actual rank of the person that served as Chief was Captain. Captain Barlow replaced Captain Robert M. Quinn, who had been Chief for 2 years.

Captain Barlow had been employed for several years at the "Mobile Register" newspaper. On January 3, 1872, the paper reported: "On Monday, Capt. W. P. Barlow, our new Chief of Police, took charge of his office, relieving Capt. Quinn, the appointee of Mayor Horst. The police force was drawn up in a hollow-square at the Guard House, and the new Chief was introduced to the officers and men. He made a short and pointed address, saying, among other things, that for the present no changes would be made, and it rested with the officers and men themselves to show, by their efficiency and zeal, that they should be retained in the positions they now fill.

"Captain Barlow has been an attaché of the Register office for a number of years, in charge of our job office, and from his sterling character, record and antecedents, which are those of a good and brave Confederate officer, we have no doubt that he will ably and efficiently fill the position entrusted to him. His appointment is a most excellent one and will give general satisfaction."

Almost immediately Chief Barlow went about upgrading the Police Department with reorganization and new equipment that was sorely needed. The first real improvement was realized on February 12, 1872, when the City Council ordered the new "circle-star" badges for the Police Officers.

Another issue that Barlow addressed immediately was the condition of police uniforms. An article appearing in the newspaper on April 17, 1872, reported:

Police Uniforms- We have frequently commented upon the shabby appearance of our police force and urged the necessity of having them properly uniformed. The matter has been held in abeyance for some time, the Boards and Police Committee being unable to agree upon a uniform, some desiring black, some blue, some gray and others none at all. The Committee a few days since, however, made a selection of a uniform consisting of a blue blouse and gray pants, which will be presented to the Boards for their approval. This uniform, though serviceable, gives dissatisfaction to many who prefer the old gray uniforms, and see no reason why it should be changed. His is a matter of preference, based upon old associations, and besides, many of the members of the old police force are already provided with the gray uniforms, and it would operate heavily upon them, pecuniarily, being men in very moderate circumstances, to compel them to discard it and buy other clothes. The gray is a good, handsome, and serviceable uniform, and the Boards should take all these facts into consideration, and by their actions do justice to a good and vigilant set of police officers, who never fail to do their duty. The old uniform is, without doubt, the preference of nearly everyone in the community.

An article appearing in the "Mobile Daily Register" on May 7, 1872, states:

Police Uniforms- The contract for furnishing the new uniforms for the police has been awarded to Mr. John Maguire, and the men were yesterday being measured, it being the intention to make the uniforms to order in a neat and serviceable manner. The clothing will be manufactured in New York, Mobile not according the necessary facilities for filling the order with dispatch.

On June 6, 1872, the "Daily Register" published the following regarding the new police uniforms.

The 'Compromise' Uniform- The police have appeared on the streets in their new 'compromise' uniforms and present such a hybrid appearance that it is hard to make them out. At first sight they look like Federal soldiers, with their blue blouses and brass buttons, but then comes the old Confederate pantaloons, and light straw hats, giving them a kind of a yankee-rebelized appearance. The police don't seem to relish the idea of being taken for members of the 2nd Infantry, not that they object particularly to the blue, which makes a serviceable uniform, but because the citizens generally joke and guy them to a great extent. Only yesterday a Private of the 2nd Infantry hailed a policeman, rigged out in his new toggery, with, "Halloa, partner, hold on a minute, and we will go to the barracks together.

The uniform could have been improved, and all gray or all blue would certainly have been better; but then some members of the Police Committee wanted blue, some gray, so they compromised matters, and the result is the present nondescript uniforms.

It would be interesting to point out at this time a very unusual city policy relating to police uniforms and equipment with the City of Mobile Police Department. Even from the very beginning back in 1835, the City required officers to supply all of their own equipment, including uniforms. Quoting from the 1835 Ordinance: "which uniform shall be furnished at the expense of the officers and men respectively, but to be made or procured under the direction of the Mayor, with such changes and alterations as he may think proper to suggest."

And further, "And be it further ordained, That the Captain and Lieutenants shall each be armed with a white mounted sword, suspended by a black Morocco or leather belt, and a brace of side pistols, to be provided at their own proper expense."

Police officers in Mobile were required to furnish their own uniforms, weapons and equipment until 1986, when William M. Mingus was appointed Chief and shortly after a new policy was implemented whereby the Police Department would furnish all uniforms and equipment.

1900-1920

1902 photograph.
Notice the framed photograph of Officer Morris (center)
who was killed in the line of duty in 1901.
This photograph is used for the book cover background.

In 1905, Edward T. Rondeau (born October 3, 1842) became the Chief of Police, replacing John Case. Rondeau had been on the Department for twenty-five years, and he served as Chief until 1909. Prior to becoming an officer, he served in the 24th Alabama Infantry Gulf City Guards. Confederate Army. He enlisted on October 17, 1861, and was discharged in Greensboro, North Carolina, on May 1, 1865. When he was replaced by Chief Vincent Giblin, he was made Chief of Detectives. Rondeau held that position until his death on July 25, 1920. He served the Mobile Police Department for over forty years.

In 1910, the Department was comprised of eighty-seven officers. This included one Chief of Police, one Chief of Detectives, two Lieutenants, two Sergeants, five Detectives, two Clerks, and sixty-five Patrolmen in addition to one each, Day Driver, Night Driver, Day Turnkey, Night Turnkey, Guard House Detail, Day Operator, Night Operator, Armorer, and Porter.

The officers worked twelve-hour shifts, seven days a week. The day shift was from 0700-1900 and night shift was from 1900-0700. Starting pay for an officer was $60 per month. The officers did not have sick pay or vacation time. If they did not work, they did not get paid. Below is the October 1910 payroll.

Chief of Police
V.A. Giblin $150.00

Chief of Detectives
E.T. Rondeau $100.00

Lieutenant
H.E. Davis $100.00
R.L. Dorlan $100.00

Sergeant
Henry Farmer $ 80.00
C.A. Schreiner $ 80.00

Detectives
C.K. Berge $ 70.00
Thomas Boltz $ 80.00
Warren Burch $ 80,00
Joe Lacey $ 80.00
J.W. Murphy $ 80.00

Patrolmen
Dave Arbo $ 60.00
George Arbo $ 60.00
F. Averyt $ 70.00
Richard A. Barrett $ 70.00

B. Bishop	$ 65.00
Ben Burch	$ 70.00
Walter Burch	$ 60.00
William Connelly	$ 60.00
William Conniff	$ 70.00
James Cottrell	$ 60.00
Frank Curry	$ 70.00
J.H. Davis	$ 70.00
Chris Dean	$ 70.00
P.A. Delahunty	$ 70.00
J.F. Demouy	$ 70.00
Thomas Doyle	$ 70.00
H.D. Evans	$ 70.00
G.E. Galle	$ 60.00
Louis Galle	$ 60.00
Thomas Gebhardt	$ 70.00
L.D. Gibson	$ 70.00
J.R. Giddens	$ 70.00
Marcus Harris	$ 60.00
Noah Harris Sr.	$ 70.00
Noah Harris Jr.	$ 60.00
Theodore Harwell	$ 70.00
F.E. Helton	$ 70.00
William Helton	$ 60.00
W.D. Humpherys	$ 70.00
J.K.P. Johnson	$ 70.00
John H. Kelly	$ 60.00
A Kennedy	$ 70.00
C.F. Lawrence	$ 60.00
C. Learman	$ 65.00
J.J. Leonard	$ 70.00
James Lewis	$ 60.00
John Lincoln	$ 70.00
R.A. Lott	$ 70.00
John Lyons	$ 60.00
J.W. Mabry	$ 60.00
H.R. Malone	$ 70.00
T.J. Mayher	$ 60.00
Alex McCarron	$ 70.00
James McGinnis	$ 70.00
James McMannis	$ 60.00

L.J. Murry	$ 70.00
Luther Murry	$ 70.00
George Ness	$ 70.00
John Ness	$ 70.00
W.V. Pearson	$ 70.00
George A. Phillips	$ 60.00
James Pistole	$ 65.00
Phil Pittroff	$ 70.00
Clyde Rayford	$ 60.00
Edward Sheets	$ 70.00
J.B. Slocum	$ 70.00
G.M. Smith	$ 60.00
E.D. Solomon	$ 60.00
A.M. Southall	$ 70.00
F. Speth	$ 70.00
W.T. Sturtevant	$ 60.00
A.G. Sutherland	$ 70.00
Joe Tucker	$ 70.00
Thomas Vegliacich	$ 65.00
J.K. Yeates	$ 60.00

Clerk

J.J. Barry	$ 80.00
Mrs. Connie Roberts	$ 50.00

Day Driver

John Bressingham	$ 70.00

Night Driver

M.D. Conniff	$ 70.00

Day Operator

L. Bauer	$ 70.00

Night Operator

George Smith	$ 70.00

Turnkey Day

Thomas Sherridan	$ 70.00

Turnkey Night

A.W. Macon	$ 60.00

Guard House Detail
W.N. Renauld $ 70.00

Armorer
W.H. Bancroft $ 70.00

Porter
Lorenzo Avery $ 50.00

"Day Force Mobile Police, Jan 10th 1911"

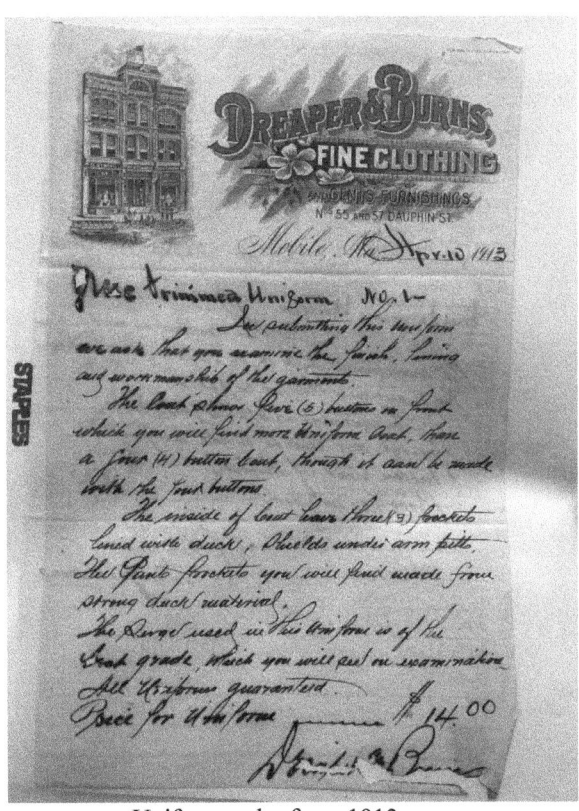

Uniform order from 1913

One of the Best in South

A "Mobile News Item" newspaper article dated October 26, 1913, gave an overview of the Mobile Police Department. It was titled "Mobile's Police Department One of the Best in South."

It states that the department numbered about one hundred men which included six detectives and the executive officers, Frank W. Crenshaw, Edward T. Rondeau, chief of detectives, Reuben Dorlan, night lieutenant, Henry Farmer, day lieutenant, Charles Schreiner, night sergeant, and Luther Murray, day sergeant.

Since assuming charge of the police department, Chief Crenshaw has been responsible for the organization of a traffic squad, composed of six men working on an eight-hour shift. He was responsible for the adoption of modern traffic ordinances which led to a decrease in the loss of life and injuries from traffic accidents. Another ordinance he was successful in passing resulted in pawn shops being required to submit daily reports of all articles pawned.

Mardi Gras postcard, February 1914,
Erik Overby Collection, University of South Alabama Archives

1916 Mobile Police Department Baseball Team
#1 Doc Brady, #2 Charlie Burton, #3 Bobby Holmes,
#4 Jake Untreiner, #5 Dick Rayford, #6 C. Marcet,
#7 Mackey White, #8 G. Woodcock, #9 Eddie Quarles,
#10 Eddie Warren, #11 Rags Lefevre

The National Police Journal, 1918

"The National Police Journal" published an article about the Mobile Police Department in April 1918. This is an interesting article as it provides some insight into the operations and manpower of the Department at that time. Additionally, it highlights Chief of Police Patrick J. O'Shaughnessy, who, as you will see in a later chapter, fell from grace.

Cover of The National Police Journal, April 1918

The Gulf City's Police Department.
By G.J. Flournoy.

The Mobile, Ala., Police department today in the matter of efficiency stands as high as any in this country. Chief of Police P.J. O'Shaughnessy's force consists of almost fifty patrolmen, and they have a wide area of territory to cover. The department does not stop at confining itself to the city limits, but on many occasions, goes to the three-mile limit to run down a violator, and even further.

All New Officers.

The Police Department of the Gulf City is what you might call new, as many of its members, in fact, the majority, never saw any police service except within the past five months. Yet there has not been one big robbery or murder committed since the department was reorganized. The department has one task that is herculean in many respects, and that is the enforcement of the prohibition law in a city and county that is composed of two-thirds local optionists. Even under these conditions the department has worked wonders, and few bootleggers venture to sell liquor here.

The personnel of the force consists of one chief, two lieutenants, two sergeants, one chief of detectives, and ten men, three chauffeurs, two motorcycle officers, one clerk who acts as assistant to the chief and in the recorder's court, two signal phone operators, two turnkeys, two detail officers at the police station, a superintendent of prisoners, a hostler, one porter, and about fifty patrolmen. There are eight traffic officers on the force.

The Mobile force has not the numerical strength demanded by a city and environment containing 80,000 inhabitants, but its present system of organization is excellent, and its service without collective fault. The increase in population and the constant changing of conditions has brought about many improvements for handling crime.

The department is equipped with a signal phone system that is modern in every respect and the men on the beats, both day and night, are required to report to headquarters every hour. The officer in charge at the station knows at all times through the location of phones on the beats, where to reach his men in the event of an emergency.

The present force, working under the personal direction of Chief O'Shaughnessy, have many important captures to their credit, and their ability has been displayed on more than one occasion. At a recent downtown fire, the work of protecting the fire fighters and the public with the quick institution of the fire lines was shown, the people being kept a block away, and although several thousand people were on the scene, no one was hurt.

Over a Century Old.

The organization of the department dates back to March 16, 1814. In that year for police purposes the township was divided into three wards, with a commissioner for each to enforce ordinances and two constables to make arrests. Fines were imposed for "allowing cows and goats to run at large," "obstructing and digging in the streets," and various other offenses which sound strange at the present time. The old records show that the salary of the first police officer was $10, quite a contrast to the present day scale. The officer with the $10 per month salary was spurred on to activity by 50 per cent. commission on fines through watchfulness. At times his renumeration must have been princely.

In 1821 police protection consisted of a city watch, in which all citizens over 16 years of age were compelled to serve. The stipend was $2 per week. The first real chief of the police (Town Marshal) was appointed on March 3, 1825. One of his tasks was the inspection of cooking and heating stoves. A small force was organized, until 1850, when it numbered thirty men and three officers. Stephen A. (sic) Charpentier was chief of police from 1851 to 1861 and had thirty-five men under him. During the war Robert T. Chamberlain was at the head of the Police Department, and at the close of hostilities in 1865Charpentier resumed command of the force.

The period during and following the Civil War was the most trying in the history of the police department. It was the days of reconstruction, and many battles were fought in the streets between whites and blacks over politics. W.W. Turner undertook the duties of chief of police in 1867, and was displaced by General Diamond (sic), a Union soldier.**(see the chapter on Chief's of Police, Dimon replaced Charpentier. Turner was chief at a later date)

During the period that the Republican party controlled the city government, R.M. Quinn and M. Barlow were at the head of the police force, which was up to 1873, as nondescript as it was possible to make it with a mixture of conditions. Theodore I. Eastburn was the first chief of police under the regained Democratic control, which was only accomplished by open warfare.

The Department's Early History.

In 1879 Col. R.P. Underhill was provisionally elected chief of police. The force was reorganized for that year, and in 1880 W.H. Williamson was named chief. In 1884 John J. Crowley was elected chief under the administration of Mayor R.B. Owen. Captain H.H. Slatter and Richard Felder followed as chiefs, and in 1894 Peter Burke was chosen head of the department, retiring with a good record in 1897. In the spring of 1897 C.W. Soost was named chief of police, and following him were Chiefs John Case, Edward T. Rondeau, Vincent Giblin, Walter F. Walsh, Frank W. Crenshaw and Gilbert M. Van Liew. The latter retired from the force on October 2, 1917, and was succeeded by the present chief, Patrick J. O'Shaughnessy.

The head of the Mobile Police Department came up from the ranks, which fact is very pleasing to the men working under him. Chief O'Shaughnessy was appointed night lieutenant and acting head of the department on October 2, 1917, and a month later he was regularly appointed chief. In the five months he has served he has worked wonders with a department that was completely reorganized at the time of his appointment, due to political conditions.

When he took office, the Federal Government was demanding that the vice district be wiped out on account of the presence of 1500 troops in Mobile. It was said that this could not be done. Even his superiors were doubtful. On an early morning in the latter part of December the people of Mobile woke up and discovered that the red light district had ceased to exist. It was no idle boast, but real facts, and the district is as clean of immorality today as the sand beaches of the Gulf coast after a storm. The chief was congratulated on all sides for his remarkable feat.

The Chief's Record.

Chief O'Shaughnessy is a native of Ireland. When 8 years of age he came to this county (sic) and settled at Bing-cated (sic) first in the public schools and later at St. James Academy. He followed the trade of cigar maker, and for a number of years traveled over the United States. He came to Mobile seven years ago and worked as a cigar maker. Later he became a member of the fire department and then resigned this work and traveled in the East selling real estate. Five years ago he joined the police force as a supernumerary, and it was not very long before he was on the regular roll. While on his beat he showed efficiency and was soon called in to act as turnkey. He was later appointed acting sergeant, and from this position was promoted to night lieutenant, and then to the command of the entire department.

Chief O'Shaughnessy is a prominent member of the Knights of Columbus, the Hibernians, is president of the Mobile Police Relief Association, and a member of the National Police Relief Association.

The Commissioner of Police in Mobile is the mayor of the city by a rule of the commission form of government. He is no other person than Hon. Pat J. Lyons, who is serving his third term as mayor under the commission form of government. As commissioner he has entire charge of the Police Department and is a regular caller at headquarters every night. He knows what is going on in the department at all times. His idea of a good police officer is one who is neat at all times, and not only useful to the city, but to the public in general.

Mayor Lyons was born in Mobile, January 17, 1850. He began life as a steamboat clerk, soon rose to chief clerk, then master and owner. He was engaged in the wholesale grocery business for many years, and in the banking business. He is interested in nearly every industrial enterprise in Mobile. He was first elected to public office in 1897 as councilman from the first ward. He ran for alderman, and for years led his ticket. He was elected president of the old city council in 1902, and in 1903 succeeded the late Charles E. McLean as mayor of the city. He was twice elected mayor and commissioner and has never known defeat.

The next officer in command to the chief of police of the Mobile department is the night lieutenant of the force. This office at the present is filled by Lieutenant Edward Sheets, a young man, in fact, the youngest man who ever held the position. While he was just promoted in October 1917, he has made good rapidly, and Chief O'Shaughnessy does not hesitate to leave him in charge of all matters when the occasion arises. He was appointed to the force on October 8, 1907, was made the market clerk in 1911 and his connection with the role of patrolman around the municipal building. It was his splendid record in this capacity that caught the eye of Mayor Pat J. Lyons. It can be truthfully said that Lieutenant Sheets won his spurs by devotion to duty.

Anet Davis and Rondeau.

Lieutenant H.E. Davis is one of the ablest assistants to Chief O'Shaughnessy. He is a stickler for promptness in his own work and in answering calls from the public. He was first appointed to the police force as a detective in 1903 under Mayor McLean and was on the force but a short time when he was named night lieutenant, serving in this capacity for four years. He left the force in 1912 of his own accord. In 1917 he returned as day lieutenant. Previous to coming to the department he was superintendent of Magnolia Cemetery. He is a native of Mobile, Ala., and is 58 years of age.

Captain Edward t. Rondeau, chief of detectives, has a remarkable record as a peace officer. He has seen service under fifteen chiefs of police, and has served as patrolman, sergeant, day and night lieutenant, and chief of police. In fact, he is the oldest man on the force, both in age and in point of service. This grand old man was a member of the police force when many were mere tots. He served the city during the days of Reconstruction, when a white man in the South wearing a police uniform took his life in his hands. Previous to joining the police force he had been a member of the gallant Twenty-fourth Alabama Regiment, Confederate States Army and no braver soldier lived. He went through four years of fighting of the real kind. He has served forty years in the department. He was born October 3, 1842. He was appointed to his present position in 1909.

There is no official in the Police Department who is as popular as "Jim" Barry, the clerk to the chief and of the recorder's court. There is no man in the city government as neat and correct with his books as this man. Although he lost his position last year through a political change, he was back on the job in less than a month's time at the urgent request of Mayor Lyons. While a very efficient official, he is never too busy to attend to the wants of the police officials, his fellow workers, the members of the bar, or the public in general. He was born in Mobile and became a member of the force on August 1, 1905.

The youngest police official in point of service is Sergeant Joseph V. Connick, whose duty is on the day shift of the department. Part of his duties takes him into the police court as assistant clerk. This young man was born in Mobile Forty-one years ago and was educated at the Christian Brothers School, and previous to taking up police work was connected with the United Fruit Company as a messenger. In this capacity he has traveled all over the United States. He served as a beat officer for eighteen months previous to being promoted to the position of sergeant.

Night Sergeant Charles A. Schreiner is one of the steadiest men on the force and has seen fifteen years of service, during which time he has been absent from duty only a few occasions. He was born in Mobile, March 27, 1855. He first began his work as a public official when he was appointed jailer of Mobile County in 1898. In the spring of 1903, he was appointed day sergeant and held this position until last October, when he was transferred to the night shift. He served as court officer of the recorder's court for many years and was very efficient. He is married and the father of seven children.

Judge D.H. Edington, presiding magistrate of the Police Court, was born July 10, 1882, at Lauderdale, Miss. He spent thirteen years at Citronelle. He was educated at the University of Alabama, graduating in the academic and law courses. He moved to Mobile in 1905 and practiced law. He entered into a partnership with Robert E. Gordon in September 1907, and both have been successful practitioners. On October 7, 1912, he was appointed city recorder and has held the position ever since. He has held office while many changes have taken place in the City Commission and when there were many hard political battles. He tries about 5000 case per year.

From left to right: Lt. H.E. Davis, Capt. E.F. Rondeau, Sgt. C.A. Schreimer, Sgt. J.V. McCormick, Clerk J.J. Barry, Lt. E.F. Sheets

Uniformed Force, Mobile Police Department

Directing Traffic is the Long Suit of These Nine Men

Mobile's, Plainclothes Squad

1920s-1930s

Patrick J. O'Shaughnessy

Patrick J. O'Shaughnessy was appointed to be Chief of Police from the ranks by Mayor Pat J. Lyons in 1917. He served as chief from then until December 1923. A Federal investigation into an illegal liquor ring led to his and seventy-one others being indicted for conspiracy to violate the national prohibition act. Prohibition in the United States was from January 17, 1920, to December 5, 1933. Alabama passed the "bone dry" act in 1915 and remained a dry state until 1937. Several officers and other city officials were implicated in the conspiracy to traffic illegal alcohol.

O'Shaughnessy was convicted with ten others and sentenced to serve two years in Federal prison. He appealed his conviction to the Court of Appeals and won a reversal. His retrial was set for April 10, 1928.

On February 2, 1928, he was beaten by J.B. and Murrell Tait, in the area of South Lawrence Street, between Canal and Palmetto Streets. He crawled to a friend's house and was taken to the hospital three days later. On February 24, 1928, he died from those injuries.

Several people were arrested who witnessed the attack and attempted to cover it up by paying the medical expenses and "other incidentals." J.B. Tait was arrested in Jonesboro, Louisiana, and extradited back to Mobile.

Below is a letter written by O'Shaughnessy to the Mayor Pat Lyons on May 9, 1918, in which he lists an assortment of seized alcohol that was destroyed by the Police Department. Of note is the last line in which he states that future seizures will be destroyed in the daytime. Based on the knowledge that O'Shaughnessy and other officers were involved in the illegal alcohol trade, it makes you wonder if the listed contraband was actually destroyed or if it was used in their illicit trade.

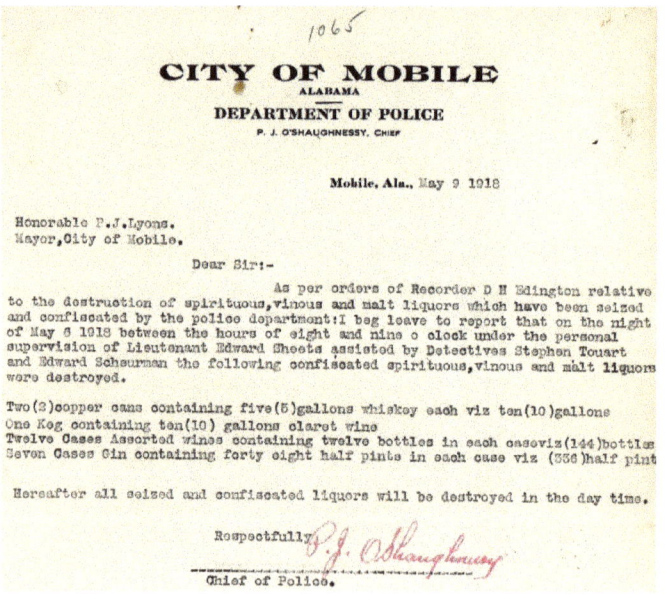

1927 Board of Commissioners Report

The 1927 Board of Commissioners Report shed some light on how the Department operated and what types of calls the officers handled.

Some highlights are:

On September 19 and 20, 1926, a storm struck Mobile and caused significant damage to the police and fire boxes. By October 5, one hundred sixty-seven fire boxes had been installed and by November 13, the police and fire signal contracts were accepted. The police department had new switchboards, battery racks and batteries installed.

Between October 1926 and September 1927, the police boxes received 110,161 regular calls and 1,052 wagon calls. The power bill for these boxes was $547.84 for the year.

Some of the arrest totals for fiscal year 1927 were:

Disorderly Conduct:	1566
Drunk:	1152
Dangerous and Suspicious:	1300
Prohibition:	448
Gambling:	452
Permitting Gambling:	2
Vagrancy:	121
Resisting and Interfering:	52
Discharging Firearms:	7
Concealed Weapons:	14
Disorderly Assembly:	41
Escape:	10
Open Store on Sunday:	10
Throughfare Ordinance:	221
Parking Ordinance:	96
Excessive Noise:	49
Passing Streetcar while Discharging Passengers:	13
Intersection Ordinance:	77
Speeding:	445
Reckless Driving:	571

Driving Car while Drunk: 87
State Auto License Law: 100
Assault and Battery: 42
Assault with a Weapon: 36
Assault with Intent to Murder: 12
Murder: 10
Manslaughter: 6
Robbery: 5
Petit Larceny: 111
Grand Larceny: 40
Burglary: 22
Rape: 2

The Police Department recovered the following stolen property that year:

138 cars...$64,820.00
Cash...$ 1,007.00
Clothing from burglaries........................$ 4,570.00
28 watches, 12 rings, 5 diamonds, 28 bicycles, 12 tires, 3 batteries, 1 package of laundry, 1 music roll, 1 spray gun, No. 2 typewriters, junk, 1 cow, 250 plumbing fixtures, 2 packages express and groceries...................$4882.00

Total Recoveries..........................$75,297.00

The total number of meals served to prisoners.....45,620.

Warren Burch submitted to the City Commission the following:

> We are comparatively free from the inroads of real crime as other cities our size, and I trust that we shall continue to hold the upper hand. However, it is my opinion, which is offered by years of experience, that the city is going to grow entirely beyond us with our present equipment and personnel. Also, that the facilities offered by this building are entirely inadequate and would highly appreciate any aid in this matter that the Board of Commissioners can possibly give. The jail itself is entirely too small, and the equipment very inadequate. I sincerely hope that along with other civic developments that the Honorable Board can see their way clear to build a modern and practical Police Station in the near future.

The building Chief Burch was talking about was the police headquarters at 57 St. Emanuel Street. It had been built in 1896 and was thirty-one-years old at the time of his writing this report. It would be another twenty-three years until the City Commissioners had a new police building constructed.

Flying Squadron

Unknown Traffic Officer; note the winged wheel
patch on his upper arm. MPD archives.

In April of 1927, the "Mobile News Item" ran a series
of articles highlighting Mobile Police Traffic Officers, the
Flying Squadron. Officer "Happy" Murphy was one of the
officers highlighted, two years prior to his murder at Broad
Street and Conti Street. Frank Green, also highlighted, passed
away while still working for the department on August 22,
1929. He had been ill for a few months after contracting a
disease while on vacation. These spotlights offer an intriguing
glimpse into the personalities of the officers, as well as the
general public opinion of them.

THE MOTORCYCLE SLEUTH

Every speed-cop isn't quite as hard as he looks on his automatic horse, as witness this glimpse of "Happy" Murphy, one of Mobile's Flying Squadron. Undoubtedly, "Happy Murphy" has just "pulled" some energetic driver, and has found him to be from the very same county on the Emerald Isle.

But, though Officer Murphy flashes such a thoroughly Irish grin, he can certainly be strict and stern upon occasion. Otherwise, he would never have made the enviable record on the Flying Squadron which he now enjoys. There is no one on the Squadron who is better than "Happy" Murphy, although there are those who are quite as good.

And, in getting to fires, Officer "Happy" Murphy is known for his agility and speed. When the fire siren blows, he heads for the

MOTORCYCLE OFFICER
"HAPPY" MURPHY

scene, and usually proceeds the trucks to the site of the conflagration, breezing along at a speed which is almost incredible.

However, at times, "Happy" Murphy loses the grin.

"There is one thing that worries me," he says. "Some day there is going to be a terrible crash between the fire trucks and some unwitting motorist who refuses to pull to the curb. It has happened before, and it's going to happen again, and in that kind of a crash, some one dies. I have tried to educate the people to pull to the curb when the siren blows, and I think I am succeeding pretty well—but there are a few left."

April 5, 1927

MADE IN MOBILE

The Made - In - Mobile movement has extended even unto the Flying Squadron of Mobile's municipal law enforcement contingent. In other words, Mobile furnishes its own motorcycle officers, and the ones that they furnish rank among the best in the squadron. There is Officer Green, for instance. Mr. Green was born and reared in Mobile. He is a motorcycle officer, he rides around on a motorcycle, he looks strict, and he makes arrests. But his arrests are made only with the best of reasons; if anyone can prove to Officer Green that the accelerator got stuck in the floor-boards, and prove it beyond the least shadow of a doubt, then that fortunate person may drive away in the direction he had intended. But if the accelerator did not

MOTORCYCLE OFFICER
GREEN

get stuck—then the unfortunate motorist will have the pleasure of Mr. Green's company back to the bastile.

Officer Green is considered one of the best additions to the Flying Squadron of Mobile in recent years. He has not worn the blue very long—two or three or four years— but, manipulating his mechanical steed with all the grace of a mounted and masculine Diana, as dapper and neat as though he had just stepped out of a band-box, and looking as though he had been melted and poured into his uniform —Mr. Green makes one of the neatest and snappiest figures of all the minions of the law in all Mobile.

April 15, 1927

136

Ex-Race Driver Motorcycle Officer

Mobile's streets may not be a race track, and a motorcycle may not have a cock-pit, but Motorcycle Officer Gene Stout, ex-race driver and well known for his ability in cramping the curves all over the country, gets just as much pleasure out of being the dare-devil of the Mobile Flying Squadron as he did out of wondering whether or not he would take the fence with him on the next stretch. Mr. Stout, youthful and handsome, is considered by the public as well as by the authorities, one of the best recent additions to the law forces of the Gulf City.

When it comes to fancy motorcycle riding, Mr. Stout is right there. And when it comes to keeping order on a thoroughfare, he is right there, too. Because, despite the attractive qualities of his typically American countenance, Officer Stout

**MOTORCYCLE OFFICER
GENE STOUT**

is stern beneath the skin. That is to say, on occasions. There are not a great many transgressors of the traffic ordinances in Mobile, but those who have the temerity to disregard the law usually hear the put-put-put of a pursuing motorcycle, and the orders to "pull to the curb", and, if it isn't Mr. Stout, it is one of his brother riders.

"Right signals," said Officer Stout, "are a great aid to traffic, and if they were used there would be about one-fourth as many accidents as there now are. I learned, while on the track, just how much it did help, and how much protection it was to one's own self, to let the man behind know what I intended to do."

April 12, 1927

137

THE MOTORCYCLE SLEUTH

MOTORCYCLE OFFICER
JACK HARPER

The pride of Mobile's Flying Squadron is Motor Cop Jack Harper, he of the feet. Officer Harper is noted for three things, his peculiar ability upon a motorcycle, his expansive array of friends in each and every station and walk of life, and his feet. It is a saying at headquarters that Jack was born upon a motorcycle, and indeed, when he spins along, weaving through traffic, to whirl and shoot back in an opposite direction without so much as an instant's hesitation, it certainly appears to have some foundation.

And speaking of foundation, so has Jack Harper. Many an amateur statistician has found his mind tottering on the verge of absolute blankness through his efforts to estimate just how far Jack's feet would reach if placed end to end.

As to friends, there are none in Mobile who do not know and like Jack, either by name or by sight—mostly by sight, because, unfortunately policemen are usually anonymous to the public. They know him by the natty fit of his uniform, his excellent handling of his machine, and his winning courtesy and smile. And they also know him by his reputation for "pulling" speeders; and therefore, knowing that the judge will never understand that they have not more time than money, they do not speed when Jack is abroad.

April 8, 1927

138

Circa 1929 photograph of parade with Traffic officers.
MPD archives.

Undated photo of Traffic Officer Gene Stout. MPD archives.

Washington Avenue and Canal Street, 1934, MPD archives.
Traffic Officer Jack Harper on left.

City of Mobile
Police Department

Mobile, Ala. July 17th 1932

Statement of Gaines Scherma,1217 Texas St

Onthe night of July ~~xxxx~~ 12th ,which was Tuesday,About 8.00 P.M.
I was setting on my gallery,with my father,mother and uncle,I saw
three boys pass on the north side of Texas,Going east to Regina Ave
They slowed up and looked around at the corner,I recognized them and
waived to them,they did not seem to recognize me for they did not
speak or waiv e either.

They continued across to the east side and went north,I dont
know how far,I could not see because it is very dark and I had no
particular reason to know

I know these boys personally, and positively state,that Ford alias
Slug West,Morris Caton and Joe Standard were the 3 boys

Gaines Scherma

Witnesses
J. V. Connick
L Arras

Witness Statement from 1932.
Witnessed by Officer Joseph V. Connick

141

1940s

The early 1940's were a difficult time in the history of the Mobile Police Department. Scandal, unprofessional, unlawful conduct by the officers, and leadership that either engaged in the improper conduct or simply ignored it led to a serious lack of trust within the community. The City Commission, comprised of three commissioners, one of which was the Mayor, had their hands full. Some positive changes were to come out of this turbulent time as we will see.

Grand Jury Investigation

On May 3, 1940, the State Solicitor of Mobile County, Bart Chamberlain, sent a letter to Mayor Cecil F. Bates and Commissioners Charles Baumhauer and Earnest Megginson outlining findings of a Mobile County Grand Jury investigation from April 1940. This letter was directed by the foreman of the Grand Jury.

During the course of the Grand Jury investigation, they found several instances of misconduct by the officers of the Mobile Police Department. Some of these are enumerated below:

It was charged that the operation of musical instruments is permitted at times prohibited by the City Ordinance. And for that privilege, the officers on the particular beat where the machine was located would be paid a sum of fifty cents per week. This amount was paid to every officer who worked the beat where the machine was located. Copies of the payments were retained by company that owned the machine and the operator of the machine. At the time, that was Bob Wheeler, who was an agent of the F.A.B. Amusement Company located at 515 Dauphin Street.

It was alleged that officers Riddle and Maples unlawfully assaulted a Black man named Eli Moore while arresting him. This complaint was actually lodged by Judge Frank Coffin, and he provided evidence to the occurrence.

It was also alleged that Officer John Casey was living with a known prostitute, Mrs. Raymond Sands. She operated a house of prostitution on St. Michael Street that had been raided by Chief Deputy Hudoff and other deputies of the Mobile County Sheriff's Office. During the raid, Casey was found in bed with Mrs. Sands. After the raid, Mrs. Sands moved her operation to 451 S. Warren Street. It was further alleged that Officer Casey drove her around town in his patrol car and on occasion, allowed her to drive it.

It was noted that the husband of Mrs. Sands was currently serving two sentences of a year and a day for two burglaries. One of the victims of a burglary had been murdered before Mr. Sands was tried. Sands was currently under indictment for that murder. It was alleged that Mrs. Sands assisted in the coverup of the murder.

Mrs. Sands was arrested for vagrancy by the Sheriff's Department and Officer Casey reported to the jail and berated the deputies for arresting her. Officer Casey would attend court with her on her cases, and it was believed that he was guiding her on concealing evidence in the murder case.

Evidence presented showed Officers Bullock and Rogers unlawfully arrested a Mr. Earl Adams who worked for the U.S. Engineers Department. During the arrest, Officer Casey was present, but no evidence was presented as to his involvement in the mistreatment of Mr. Adams. Evidence was presented that during the arrest, Officers Bullock and Rogers knocked Mr. Adams to the ground, beat him with fists and a club, and stole his wallet that contained $23.00. This was witnessed by multiple people who testified.

On March 30, 1940, Mr. and Mrs. Robert Culpepper were riding in their car, westbound on St. Francis Street. As they approached Cedar Street or Warren Street, Mr. Culpepper suffered a heart attack. He was transported to the City Hospital where he died. Officers Bullock and Casey arrived at the hospital where they searched the body of Mr. Culpepper. After they departed, it was discovered that between $65 and $75 was missing from the body. Seven witnesses could testify to the actions of the two officers. It was further noted that they had made a complaint at Police Headquarters, and the officer in charge became indignant.

The Grand Jury would investigate various charges that it was common practice to search prisoners at the police station where officers would take personal items from prisoner's pockets and keep them.

Evidence was presented that Mr. Dudley McFadyen, an investigator with the Alcoholic Beverage Control Board (McFadyen would become Chief of Police in October 1941 and remain in that position until October 1961), was under a house occupied by Negro bootleggers, where he was waiting on a keg of moonshine to be delivered. Also present for this undercover operation were Alcoholic Beverage Control Board Detective Fountain and Mobile County Sheriff's Deputy Hargett. Fountain and Hargett were in an unmarked car, parked a short distance from the house but with direct sight. Two Mobile Police Officers drove up in a marked patrol car and saw the undercover men as they sat in the car. The two officers then drove to the house and told the occupants that they needed to look out since there were State agents in the neighborhood. This tipoff was heard by the unseen McFadyen.

I can find no further information on the Grand Jury investigation, and it is unclear what became of the individual officers or the cases in which they were involved. What is clear is that there was a pattern of misconduct that permeated the ranks of the Mobile Police Department in the late 1930s and early 1940s. Changes would be made but not before another scandal rocked the Department and the community.

40 Officers Arrested

In early October 1940, forty Mobile Police Officers were indicted by a Federal Grand Jury on a charge of Conspiracy to Violate the Internal Revenue Laws of the United States. This conspiracy was alleged to center around the acceptance of bribes to turn a blind eye to bootleggers or to actually assist them in their criminal activities. On October 7, 1940, the first five officers were arrested followed by eleven more on October 8, and fourteen on October 9.

At the time of the arrests, the Mobile Police Department had one hundred fifteen officers. Having a third of the department arrested, including ten of the eleven detectives and both plainclothes officers assigned to the detective bureau, twelve of the twenty scout car officers and sixteen of the fifty-eight patrolmen on the Department caused a near shutdown of operations. Applications and testing for police officer positions was rushed, and on October 10, eleven new officers were appointed. To better handle the calls for service, Chief Emory Warren put the Department on two twelve-hour shifts.

On October 28, former detective James Quina pleaded guilty. His sentencing was postponed until after the trial and sentencing of the other officers. Another officer, George Crawford, was granted a severance from the group being tried because he was homebound due to an injury he sustained after being struck by a motor vehicle while on duty. The remaining thirty-eight officers would be tried together in the Federal Court.

On November 25, 1940, the trial began in District Judge John McDuffie's courtroom. The prosecutor was District Attorney Francis H. Inge. The defendants were represented by George A. Sossaman and D.R. Coley, Jr. The prosecution called seventy witnesses.

On December 4, 1940, officers Leslie Ellis and Charles Burton were exonerated, and all charges against them dropped. The two officers were put back on the rolls of the Police Department.

During the trial, witnesses testified that two of the defendants sold One hundred twenty-five gallons of "shinny" (moonshine) to a bootlegger for $125. They alleged that the moonshine was delivered in a police vehicle. Officers were accused of providing protection to a female bootlegger for weekly payoffs. The amounts of the payoffs varied, depending on what was being protected. Some payoffs were fifty cents, others $2, but the sum could be as high as $22 per week or in one instance $50 for having an officer turn over an impounded car with a load of whisky in it. In that case, the witness stated that he paid the officer on the side of the police building and was handed the keys to his vehicle which he promptly drove from the police parking lot.

On December 11, 1940, the jury convicted ten of the accused and acquitted the remaining twenty-six. The convicted officers were sentenced that day. The ten men who were convicted are:

Elijah Blackmon, sentenced to 18 months.

James Bullock, sentenced to 18 months.

Joseph Casey, sentenced to 18 months.

Leroy Flake, sentenced to 1 year and 1 day.

James Lefevre, sentenced to 18 months.

Richard Lincoln, sentenced to 24 months.

Morris Pollard, sentenced to 18 months.

Claude Rayford, sentenced to 1 year and 1 day.

Francis Scanlan, sentenced to 18 months.

Eugene Tillman, sentenced to 18 months.

The ten who were convicted were released on a $1,000 appeal bond.

The twenty-six officers who were acquitted of the conspiracy charges were, James Barrett, Walter Burch, Edgar

Carney, Joseph Clark, Joseph V. Connick, Cordell Danzy, Lawrence Durden, Joseph Essler, Antonio Franco, Sam Hyland, Arthur Kirkland, Leon Kopf, Dennis Lynch, Marshall Maples, Jules Marcet, Sledge Medicus, Lorenzo Miller, Henry Milton, Paul Nelce, James Nicholas, Frederick Olsen, William Puckett, Charles Riddle, Lawrence Shaw, Edmund Tunstall, and Malcolm White.

On December 16, 1940, the City Commission, through Mayor Cecil M. Bates, issued a letter to the press and public, outlining the unanimous decision of whether to re-instate the twenty-six acquitted officers to the Police Department. The commission determined that the officers should remain fired from the employment of the City of Mobile. It states in part:

On December 12th, the Petit Jury trying the case returned a verdict convicting ten of the remaining defendants and acquitting twenty-six.

The question is now presented to the City Commission as to whether or not the twenty-six officers who were acquitted should be restored to duty as members of the Police Department. The Commission has given most careful study to the issue presented in the trial of the Government's case, of the defense presented by the officers indicted and to the testimony offered during the course of the trial and has considered most carefully its responsibility as the governing body of the City of Mobile and its duty to the citizens of this City.

It should be borne in mind that the charge on which these men were tried was one of conspiracy, not bribery, it being the theory of the Government that the officers had joined together in a mutual undertaking and with a common understanding for the protection of bootleggers from arrest and prosecution.

The direct charge on which they were tried was not that of bribery or the acceptance by an individual officer of a bribe for his failure to perform his duty. It was one of the theories of the defense, clearly shown throughout the course of the trial, that while each of the individual defendants may have himself accepted a bribe, in so doing he was acting for himself alone and not in conjunction with the others. This line of defense was based upon an accepted principle of law. The jury trying this case could have believed from the evidence that each of the defendants was guilty of accepting a bribe, but yet it would have been its duty to acquit each of the defendants if it did not believe a conspiracy existed between them.

The verdict of the jury acquitted twenty-six of the defendants of the conspiracy charge. The duty of the commission is now to determine whether any or all of these men were shown by the evidence presented in that case to be guilty of accepting a bribe, neglecting their duty or otherwise guilty of conduct unbecoming an officer.

The Government, in presenting its case, placed upon the stand thirty-six witnesses. Each one of them testified as to either having paid a bribe to one or more of the officers on trial, or had seen such a bribe paid to them. Other than entering a plea of Not Guilty in the beginning of the trial, very little, if any, evidence was presented by the defense in denial of the direct testimony offered by the Government.

The Commission further feels that it is its duty to see that the members of the Police Department perform their duties in an honest and impartial manner, and that the officers of the Department should at all times so conduct themselves as to remain above public suspicion. As a result of its study of this entire case, the Commission has reached the conclusion that the twenty-six officers who were acquitted, as well at the ten who were convicted, were guilty of neglect of duty and of *conduct unbecoming to an officer and that they should be discharged from the services of the City, effective December 12th, 1940.*

The document was signed by Mayor Bates and Commissioners Charles Baumhauer, and Earnest M. Megginson.

The dismissed officers were afforded the right to appeal their termination to the Civil Service Board, where Personnel Director Harry Pillans would make a determination as to whether a public meeting should be granted. By December 21, 1940, all twenty-six officers who had been acquitted but fired had filed appeals.

On December 27, 1940, the newspaper published the names of thirty-two men who had been hired to replace the dismissed forty. Among these new hires was a man named Talley Rollings who became the Chief of Police from October 1961 to July 1963.

Inspector of Police Arthur Thalacker

After news of the Grand Jury indictments against forty members of the Police Department and in conjunction with the mountain of evidence of misconduct by members of the department, the City Commission felt it was necessary to make some changes.

On October 11, 1940, the City Commission requested the Personnel Board create a position of Inspector of Police. On that same day, the position was created, for a one year timeframe with a monthly salary of between $350 and $450. The following specifications were adopted as to the persons applying for the position:

He shall make a complete study of the organization, procedure, personnel, equipment, and the facilities of the police department, having for this purpose full authority to obtain any information he deems relevant; he shall make recommendations to the City Commission for the improvement of the department; as the highest ranking man in the department, he shall have full authority to make changes in organization and procedure, supervise training of personnel, and take other steps to improve the morale and efficiency of the police force, and shall do related work as required.

A search was conducted to fill the position and on November 8, 1940, the job was offered to Arthur W. Thalacker. J. Edgar Hoover, the Director of the FBI made two recommendations for the position. The first was unavailable, so it was agreed by the City Commission and Personnel Director that "the second best man in the country" would be their pick. The Civil Service Board even waived the normal testing procedures for a civil service position. Mr. Thalacker was the Chief of Police in Burlington, Vermont. and prior to that, he was a police detective in White Plains, New York. He attended the 4th class of the FBI National Academy which graduated on April 3, 1937. While a detective in White Plains, he opened a training school for policemen in the area towns and counties. The training schools were well received, with nearly 80 departments in the surrounding area applying. On November 10, 1940, Arthur Thalacker accepted the position.

On Wednesday, November 27, 1940, Arthur Thalacker arrived in Mobile and took control of the Mobile Police Department. As could be expected, he was not well received in Mobile by the current Chief of Police, Emory Warren, or by many of the veteran officers on the Department. Some of the conflict between him and Chief Warren could be attributed to the conduct of the parties during the first meeting in Mayor Bates' office. A letter to Mr. Thalacker from Mayor Bates, dated July 21, 1941, sheds light on the discord between Thalacker and Warren. It states that during the first meeting, Mr. Thalacker stated that he had not yet decided if Chief Warren was guilty of the same charge on which certain Mobile Police officers were being tried. Thalacker stated that until such time as he did find him guilty, he would accept him upon the basis the Commission asked. There was probably no way to recover from that misstep, and the relationship between the two never improved.

Despite the self-inflicted damage to his leadership and the lack of cooperation from the veteran officers and leaders, Mr. Thalacker did make some improvements to the department. In short order, he identified serious failures and discrepancies in how the department operated and how the men were trained.

Thalacker created a Police Training School for officers, much like the ones he created in New York, that were well attended by new hires or less senior police officers. Attendance was voluntary, and it operated at no cost to the City. It was conducted on Mondays and Tuesdays for a period of two-and-a-half hours. These classes provided training that would take years to learn while walking the beat.

Mr. Thalacker wanted to create a new Identification Bureau, so he established a special school to learn about fingerprints. Again, it was a volunteer training program that was attended while off duty. In a short time, ten officers were trained and were qualified as experts with the exception of courtroom testimony and the development of latent prints.

Another class was a School of Detection of Crime. Twelve men were selected to attend the inaugural class, and they were taught "every phase of police work." He stated that he wanted to conduct the class with a small number of students so he could give more attention to their individual problems, and in cases of emergency, there would still be plenty of officers available for response.

The telephone/communications system was found to be flawed. He discovered that in cases of emergency, the department could not operate efficiently. There was no centralization within the Department to receive complaints by telephone. The department had four telephone numbers listed, but if no one was present to answer the phones, the call would go unanswered. It was common to have no officers available to answer the phone when court was in session. He changed the way the department operated by centralizing the phones in one station, and he had three trunk lines installed to handle the incoming call load.

As noted earlier, there had been accusations of abuse and thievery by officers who were working in the docket room. Mr. Thalacker discovered this as well, and he changed the way booking procedures were handled. Upon his appointment, the docket or booking room was in the rear of the police building, under the City Jail. Thalacker had this moved to the front of the police building, outside of the Chief's office. Three lieutenants were placed in charge of the room. Sergeants were removed from the position and placed back on the street to better observe the beat officers. All persons arrested would now come before one of the lieutenants for booking, with the exception of those who were too intoxicated. The lieutenant was required to keep a record of all of the activities of the department that were recorded in a book and any property removed from a prisoner was recorded and kept under the control of the lieutenant.

He reorganized the record bureau so the Department could keep an accurate record of all its business, listing the number of complaints, types of crimes, offense reports, and follow-up reports. The bureau would also keep a pawnbroker file, master arrest file, property file, and a file according to location of crime. He added a map that divided the city into thirteen districts that was used to track criminal activity by location in an effort to better understand trends and be able to respond quickly to any developing patterns of criminal activity. An additional map was created to track traffic accidents in the city. He implemented the use of cards to record pawned property, stolen property, or recovered property as a way to quickly research and compare items.

His goal was to have the most-detailed informational file in the county. The information would be recorded in four searchable ways: by location, type of crime, property serial number, or names. Additionally, he created the use of a 3 x 5-inch card for identifying any person who was brought to the attention of the department. This card is still in use today and is known as a Field Information Card. This card is invaluable for identifying suspects or persons of interest. He obtained the assistance of the FBI in inaugurating the files.

As stated earlier, Mr. Thalacker wanted to create an Identification Bureau. This was implemented in the spring and early summer of 1941 with the goal of keeping records on persons, including fingerprints, as part of the National Defense Program. This program oversaw the war production in the United States. Although we were not yet at war, President Franklin D. Roosevelt implemented the program to ensure we would be ready if and when the United States was brought into the conflict. As part of the program, an identification card system was implemented that would collect and maintain information of job applicants. The information obtained included a photograph, demographic information, and fingerprints; and it was used to document the background of the civilian workforce at any plant or facility in the production of war materials. The Alien Registration Act of 1940 required all non-citizen adults to register with the Federal government in the hopes of identifying subversives and spies (the "Fifth Column"), but by 1941, immigrants and citizens alike were required to submit to background checks to work on defense projects. Copies of the registration cards and all fingerprint cards were collected and stored by the Identification Bureau. Mr. Thalacker wrote to the mayor on May 9, 1941 that the Department received an average of one hundred twenty-five cards per day which were forwarded to the FBI for comparison. He noted that of the seven hundred fifty fingerprint cards already forwarded to the FBI, three hundred sixty-nine individuals were identified with criminal histories.

Another use of the records-keeping was to assist with the investigations into possible members of the Fifth Column. The term is used for subversives who work behind the scenes to undermine a government or country in the hopes of destabilizing them in a time of war. In 1941, the Fifth Column was comprised of Nazi sympathizers and propagandists. On May 26, 1940, President Roosevelt, in a radio speech, condemned persons who closed their eyes to what was happening in Europe, and he warned of a potential threat to American security by "the Fifth Column that betrays a nation unprepared for treachery." During this time in history, police departments across the country were obtaining and keeping files on persons suspected of treachery. In the 1940s, it was the Nazi who was being sought; in the 1950s. it was the communist.

A Prostitution File was created to assist the Health Department in curbing the outbreak and spread of gonorrhea and syphilis. This was a widespread problem in the area and with all of the soldiers in Mobile, it was spreading beyond the city. The prostitute file consisted of a fingerprint, photograph, and demographic information, and it was kept in a separate file cabinet. The prostitute was also required to have a health card. This card had the prostitute's demographic information and picture. On the reverse, there were lines for the date of medical examinations to be filled in by a physician. The doctor's certificate was not provided to the individual prostitute but was forwarded to the Health Department which then forwarded it to the Police Department. If a prostitute was found to be positive for gonorrhea or syphilis, she would be brought to police headquarters. It was noted that during the initial two weeks of the program, three cases of gonorrhea had been discovered. In conjunction with this identification program, the Department began documenting locations of prostitution and the prostitutes who worked in each area. Officers began investigating individuals for violations of the White Slave Traffic Act of 1910, better known as the Mann Act—a Federal law that criminalized the transportation of any woman or girl across state lines for the purpose of prostitution or debauchery or for any other immoral purpose. By May 1941, there were one hundred fifty registered prostitutes in the City of Mobile.

In January 1941, the Mobile Police Department had four detectives. By May 1941, that number increased to twelve and a Detective Bureau was established. Thalacker stated in a letter to the Commission, that Chief Warren was in direct supervision of the detectives, but that due to the lack of proper supervision, he was making changes. He wanted to appoint two sergeants and a lieutenant to the bureau. The lieutenant would supervise the day shift and the sergeants would supervise the night shift.

Burglary, Vice, and Narcotics Squads were created and operational by May 1941. With the creation of these squads, burglary and robbery files were created.

A National Defense File was created for the investigations into Nazis, communists, and those individuals detrimental to our internal security and forwarded to the Department by the FBI. One detective was assigned to investigate all persons who were identified by the FBI. By May 1941, twenty-five people had been identified and investigated. Mr. Thalacker stated that one of the biggest hinderances to the proper investigation of the suspects was the lack of a vehicle for the investigator.

He ordered the city jail to fingerprint every person brought into the jail, and they were not allowed to make bail until the fingerprint cards were completed. And with those changes, he implemented searches of mail and packages delivered to prisoners to ensure contraband or escape implements were not brought into the jail.

He created a secure file on all confidential informants. Prior to this, individual officers would use a source as they saw fit and on occasion, unethical or illegal use of informants was discovered. Under the new policy, all informants were documented and protected. The file contained nearly two hundred fifty people.

A Wanted File of Criminals was created on April 27, 1941. This file contained information on wanted suspects as reported by the FBI and state agencies. It contained fingerprint files that could be compared to fingerprints of prisoners or those working on National Defense Programs. By May 9, 1941, three wanted suspects were apprehended.

The Mobile Police Department had a standard uniform in place, though it had changed several times since the mid-1860s. Mr. Thalacker discovered that officers were purchasing uniforms that did not meet the standards or requirements of the existing uniform policy. Officers were buying uniforms in their preferred style. He implemented strict policies in obtaining and wearing the authorized uniform.

A book of "Rules and Regulations" was created to govern the conduct of the members of the Mobile Police Department. This book also dictated procedures on handling certain types of cases. The document was eighty-three pages long and was submitted to the City Commission, and City Attorney to determine if any of the rules were in conflict with existing state law or local ordinance. The book was also given to the Civil Service Board for their approval.

On September 18, 1941, Mr. Thalacker wrote to the City Commission his recommendations for improving the Department in the upcoming fiscal year. He states that his recommendations should be followed regardless if he was retained as Inspector of Police after November 27th.

Among his recommendations were an improved salary scale and other improvements. He asked for a new classification for two department stenographers to assist the detectives, the creation of four captains, one additional lieutenant, six additional sergeants, six additional detectives, twenty-five additional patrolmen, four policewomen, two clerks, six wards and one police matron. He asked for annual pay increases of $5 but only if the employee had high marks on his merit sheet. The merit sheets were implemented under Thalacker's direction.

Mr. Thalacker recommended creating a "three-platoon" system. This would improve the working conditions for the officers. At time of his writing, officers were required to work seven days a week. If he wanted to take a day off, he had to report sick or take time off without pay. Under the three-platoon system, officers would be given one day off each week. He noted that there were eleven men on the department who had not reported to work for several months to up to two years, but they were still receiving their monthly salaries. He recommended firing these officers and amending the rules and regulations of the Civil Service Board that allowed the abuse of the sick leave.

He also recommended allocating $175 in the budget to send the Inspector of Police to the FBI Re-training School.

The proposed pay scale for the Police Department is as follows:

Classification	Minimum	Maximum
Chief of Police	$300	$350
Captains	$250	$275
Jail Warden	$250	$275
Chief Clerk	$225	$250
Lieutenants	$225	$250
Sergeants	$200	$225
Detectives	$175	$200
Radio Operator	$150	$175
Patrolmen	$150	$175
Policewomen	$125	$150
Police Matron	$125	$150
Secretary	$100	$125
Clerk	$100	$125
Stenographer	$100	$125
Prison Guards	$100	$125
Janitor	$80	$100

By September 20, 1941, a letter from Thalacker to Mayor Bates stated the working relationship between Thalacker and Chief Warren had not improved. If anything, it had deteriorated to the point that something had to be done. Chief Warren's behavior did not go unnoticed outside of the department. His actions during investigations into the forty indicted police officers in 1940 was alarming, and it was reported to Mr. Thalacker in correspondence from Mr. J. Mack Eaton of the Treasury Department, Internal Revenue Service, Alcohol Tax Unit.

On July 21, 1941, Mr. Eaton wrote Mr. Thalacker a letter expressing his observations and concerns during an interview with Chief Warren on September 21, 1940. The interview was conducted in Chief Warren's office at Police Headquarters. Eaton states that during the interview, Warren told him that only active officers on the police force were implicated in the investigation by the U.S. Government because the others who were not implicated were too old or too lazy to go out and make money.

Chief Warren blamed the City of Mobile for the fact that officers were taking money from bootleggers because of the low pay they received as salary. He also stated that his interest in police work was stopping crimes such as rape, robbery, confidence men, etc., not in liquor.

Eaton further states that Warren told him that one of the men implicated, Scanlon, was one of his best men. This statement was made by Warren before Scanlon had been implicated. This gave suspicion that Warren was well aware of the misdeeds and criminal activity of the men on his Department.

Chief Warren did state in the interview that he had told the officers on the Department that if he ever got evidence of them collecting money, he would fire them.

The letter dated September 20, 1941, from Thalacker to Mayor Bates led to an additional letter that was sent on September 30, 1941, from Thalacker to Mayor Bates. In this letter, it reiterated the information that was in the September 20 letter, but it also enumerated seven allegations of misconduct or insubordination by Chief Warren. They are as follows:

On January 15, 1941, Chief Warren was ordered to investigate and report to Inspector Thalacker concerning alleged misappropriation of traffic fines collected. On February 11, 1941, Chief Warren, having made no report, again was asked for same. To date, no report on the matter from Chief Warren.

On March 6, 1941, Chief Warren instructed to report once each day to discuss with the Inspector all police matters coming via mail to the department. To date: Neither instruction followed.

On February 11, 1941, Chief Warren instructed to make investigation and to report his findings on gambling and lotteries. On April 19, May 10th and June 7th, Chief Warren was advised of specific instances necessitating investigation with instructions to make arrests or seizures of equipment, or in any event report back to Inspector. To date: Nor report or arrest concerning any of the specific complaints, no general effort to deal with the lottery situation on the part of the Chief. When lottery ordinance passed, Inspector instructed Chief to handle. Chief turned the matter over to Lieutenant Schottgen, who with the aid of Inspector and men of lottery squads, proceeded to deal with the situation.

Chief Warren also instructed to leave information in the Docket Room concerning where he could be found in case he was wanted and to report on time sheet time of his entry and leaving of the building. Among several specific occasions, when he failed to leave such information, which were detrimental to departmental efficiency, the following are reported.

April 29, 1941, 2:30 pm. Unable to locate, regard to strike situation.

April 30, 1941, 1:30 pm. Unable to locate, in regard to the death of Officer Marcet.

On June 26, 1941, Chief Warren again was instructed concerning rules for his reporting.

To date: Chief Warren leaves occasional information as to his whereabouts when away from the building, and as to his arrival and departure.

On May 29, 1941, Chief Warren called upon interdepartmental telephone by Inspector and instructed to meet Inspector in his office the next day at 2:30 pm concerning sabotage threat. Inspector waited until 6:45 pm the afternoon of May 30th, 1941, for Chief to fill appointment. Chief Warren did not report.

Chief Warren failed to follow instructions from the Inspector in regard to his assigned duty to reorganize the Detective Department. Inspector having to handle this detail and not being able to give the proper time.

Chief Warren failed to follow instructions from the Inspector in regard to the duties assigned to him about the problem of prostitution and in particular with regard to the effect of this problem on National Defense. Instructions were made to Chief Warren in the light of Major Leasure recommendations. Later, on June 26, 1941, Chief Warren instructed to prepare a daily sheet concerning the activities of the Department regarding the handling of this matter and the other matters that come to the attention of the Police Department and report same to the Inspector daily. To date: Chief Warren has made no report concerning any of the matters.

This letter was supplemental to letters submitted by Inspector Thalacker to Mayor Bates on June 27, July 22, and September 22, 1941. It obviously got the attention of the City

Commission because on October 3, 1941, Chief Warren was ordered to attend a hearing in the Council Chamber at City Hall on October 7, 1941 at 2:30 pm for the purpose of hearing the charges filed against him. Chief Warren was replaced as Chief of Police by Dudley McFadyen that month.

Dudley McFadyen

Dudley McFadyen was appointed as Chief of Police in October 1941. He held that position until October 1961, serving as Chief of Police longer than any other chief in the Department's history.

When McFadyen took command of the Department, there were eighty-six officers. The Department had been decimated by the arrests and firing of the corrupt officers previously mentioned. When he retired twenty years later, he had built the Department to over three hundred officers.

In 1946 McFadyen instituted a rotation list for wreckers and ambulances operating in the City of Mobile. Prior to this, wreckers and ambulances from different companies would race to the scene of traffic accidents or other calamities in an effort to be first on scene to get the job. He oversaw the upgrades to the communications systems, patrol cars and equipment, and uniforms. He was widely regarded as the chief who made the Department the professional organization that it is today.

Dudley McFadyen was so loved by his subordinates that when he submitted his resignation letter for retirement, one hundred ninety of his officers, including staff officers, signed a petition to the City Commissioners to keep him on as the Chief of Police.

McFadyen began his career in 1927, with the Mobile County Sheriff's Office. In 1930 he began working for the State of Alabama as an alcohol officer. Upon leaving the Mobile Police Department after twenty years as chief, McFadyen became the Chief Criminal Investigator for the Mobile County Sheriff's office. He held that position for six years. Dudley McFadyen passed away on May 14, 1976, at the age of seventy-seven.

Random Tidbits from the 1940s

In December 1947, the Department increased the minimum height and weight requirements for men seeking positions on the Department. Previously, the minimum height and weight for applicants were 5 feet 7 inches tall and 135 pounds. The new minimum standards were 5 feet 9 inches tall and 145 pounds. This change was recommended by the City Commissioners.

In January 1948, the Department was placed under a standardized set of rules and regulations. These rules and regulations were the first formal standardized rules for the Department. The rules and regulations were drafted by Chief Dudley McFadyen and his subordinates following several months of study. They were reviewed by the City Attorney and the Mayor and after their approval, the rules given to the City Commission for review and approval. These rules set forth the duties and responsibilities of every employee of the police department. They were the first of what would become the Mobile Police Department General Orders.

In September 1948, the department scheduled the installation of a new radio system. The department's current outdated system would be inoperable by July 1, 1950, the date in which the FCC mandated a frequency change for the police radios.

The City agreed to purchase $25,000 in new equipment that included dispatch equipment for two locations and radios in patrol cars. The main dispatch station would be located in Police Headquarters at 57 St. Emanuel Street, and the backup would be at the Springhill station. The system switched from the AM frequency to the FM frequency. A radio telegraph transmitter was also purchased and installed which allowed the department to communicate with all major police departments in the country.

On January 16, 1948, the "Mobile Register" published an article by Ted Pearson that told the story of how the radios installed in Mobile Police cars were wreaking havoc in Idaho Falls, Iowa. Apparently, the radio frequencies being used at that time, when transmitted by the fifteen-watt transmitters in the patrol cars, experienced a phenomenon known as "sky wave," which would bounce the radio traffic from Mobile to Iowa where it was picked up by that city's police department. That agency was inundated with our radio traffic to the point where they could not obtain airtime to transmit their own traffic to each other. This radio interference was also experienced by Mobile Police officers as well, only they were being inundated with calls from California.

Mardi Gras circa 1940.
Traffic Officer Ed Turner on left, Officer Bill Thompson on right.

1942 Motorcycle Officers Reeves, Gibney, Paine, Turner,
Eubanks, and Thompson.

1945 Female Traffic Officers

First Row: Officer John Clark, Officer Tony Bardisch, Sgt. Travis Scott, Lieut. George Lundy, Detective Douglas Thompson, Detective Joseph Burch, Officer George Lambert. Second Row: Detective William Stuckey, Officer Ivan Swift, Officer Marion Soufule, Officer Fairins Morgan, Officer Leslie B. Sisle, Officer Sidney Mills, Officer Harry Clemens. Third Row: Officer Henry Wilson, Officer Ralph Johnson, Officer Ed Adams, Officer Michael Cawith, Officer John J. Harvey, Officer Lloyd Flowers, Officer Donald Riddle. Fourth Row: Officer Horace Waldo, Officer William M. Riley, Officer Harry Rogers, Officer Howard Brown, Officer Siegfried Barnes, Officer Edward Powers. Fifth Row: Officer Jules McNellage, Officer Harry B. Ward, Officer Morris Dulaney, Officer Jesse Nabks, Officer George McGunagle, Officer Joseph A. Wade.

1945 Day Shift

164

First Row: Lieut. Robert Banks, Capt. Talley Rawlings, Miss Rowena Stewart, Officer Charles Donaldson, Officer Ollie White, Officer Jack Nelson, Officer Russell Campbell, Officer Fritz Meriwether, Officer Zeno Ryehan, Officer Harold Kirkland, Miss Valmia Dumas, Sgt. Jay C. Coker, Chief Dudley E. McFayden. Second Row: Capt. Ed J. McLean, Detective James J. Robinson, Detective Clarence Barclay, Officer John Hare, Officer June McLamore, Officer Bun Craven, Officer Obie Mealroy, Officer Herbert Smith, Officer Walter Lavere, Officer Sam Bartlett, Detective Walter Burch, Detective Francis Funk, Officer William Lann. Third Row: Gustave Huss, Officer George Houston, Officer Thos. Ludam, Officer James E. Haynes, Officer Clayton Manley, Officer Grester Dumas, Officer Otis Dees. Fifth Row: Officer Milford Nicholson, Officer Thomas Brown, Officer Arthur Whitehead, Officer Wade Creech, Officer William P. Mack. Sixth Row: Officer Dewey Core, Officer Wilfred Maddox, Officer Lawrence Wellbrook, Officer Noah Jacobs, Officer Ralph Jordan, Officer Thomas Norman. Seventh Row: Officer Leslie Manchew, Officer Ambrose Shelton, Officer George Winstanley, Officer Randall Jordan, Officer Patrick Gibney, Officer J. B. Robinson.

1945 Evening Shift

First Row: Detective Robert Sasseman, Detective John R. Brunson, Lieut. John C. Ard, Sgt. Leo Staidher, Detective Francis Slade, Detective Arthur T. Fields. Second Row: Officer Ed Bartlett, Lawrence Booker—Steward, Officer Oliver Harwell, Officer Charley Nall, Officer Elvin Weston, Officer Charles Wimberly, Officer M. C. Rigsby, Officer Fred Walters, Officer Bruce Etheridge, Officer John J. Smith. Third Row: Officer Jack Clark, Officer Lambert Barrett, Officer Milton Watts, Officer Hugh Price, Officer Jane J. Williamson. Fourth Row: Officer Joseph Law, Officer Emmett DeMouy, Officer Horace Lackler, Officer A. W. Corry, Officer Ed Turner. Fifth Row: Officer William, Officer Barney Bray, Officer Alvin Ramsey, Officer Maurice Wiggins, Officer Daniels Eagerton. Sixth Row: Officer Otto Zundel, Officer Robert Pearson, Officer John J. Hickman, Officer Oscar Slay, Officer William Simmons, Officer Allen Fore, Officer Wendell Stowe.

1945 Night Shift

1948. Obtained from the Minnie Mitchell Archives, Mobile Historic Preservation Society. Notice the different badges worn by the officers and the sergeant standing in the doorway.

December 4, 1949 at Bates Field
Ed Turner, Bill Thompson, Lt. Edwin Tuthill, and unknown female.

1950s

The 1950s started with the officers of MPD being the lowest paid in the region. A "Press Register" study found that a patrolman in Mobile made between $181-$208 per month compared to $200-240 in Montgomery, $250 in Nashville, $218-$260 in Atlanta, and $190-$240 in New Orleans. Sergeants in Mobile made between $208-$238 compared to $240-$276 in Montgomery, $280 in Nashville, $274 in Atlanta, and $230-$270 in New Orleans. Lieutenants in Mobile made between $238-$272 compared to $264-$300 in Montgomery, $305 in Nashville, $309 in Atlanta, and $250-$290 in New Orleans.

The Civil Service System (which would become the Mobile County Personnel Board) had been in existence for ten years at this time and still not a single officer was at the maximum pay step for his rank.

In October 1950, the City adjusted the pay for the Police Department. This brought the average for patrolman from $192 to $203, but they did not adjust the steps, so fifty-eight patrolmen were now maxed out at $208 per month. There was not much to look forward to in regard to improved salaries for the rank and file.

In April 1950, the Department moved from their old Headquarters and jail at 57 St. Emanuel Street to the newly built, modern headquarters building at 51 Government Street. The Department had been in the old building since the spring of 1897 after moving from the original guard house building at 29 Conti Street between Royal and St. Emanuel Streets. The old headquarters was opened fifty-three years earlier, and there were only two men still alive that took part in the move. One was Officer John Bressingham who, at this time, was hospitalized in serious condition, and retired Officer George Flournoy who was currently a circuit court bailiff.

In July 1950, the City Commission passed an ordinance that banned police and fire unions. After the ban was placed into effect, officers and firemen were required to sign a document that stated they were no longer affiliated with a union. Twenty-seven officers and firemen were fired for refusing sign the document. They filed a lawsuit against the City. In May 1954, the City rescinded the ordinance after the Alabama Supreme Court ruled that a portion of the ordinance was unconstitutional, and the other portions were under review. The City began negotiating the return of the twenty-seven fired employees. The Personnel Board began sending letters to the fired employees offering them the opportunity to sign up for re-employment list based on their seniority when they were fired. They were also sent a form to fill out and sign if they did not wish to be re-employed with the city. The reappointments were not automatic and guaranteed. The officers were placed on a hiring list that would be pulled from when vacancies opened.

In January 1954 the Department was reorganized into five divisions. The new divisions were Administration, headed by Captain Ed McLean; Detective, headed by Captain Talley Rollings; Traffic, headed by Captain Edwin Tuthill; Uniform, headed by a to-be-named Captain; and Communications, headed by Chief Communications Officer Howard Black. Additionally, the Department moved Sergeant Walter Dumas from the Traffic Division to Training. He assumed training duties for the Department under the supervision of Captain Rollings.

Talley Rollings

With the new reorganization, a new captain position was created for the Uniform Division, a lieutenant position for the Detective Division, and a new sergeant position to replace Sergeant Dumas who was moved to the training position.

Talley Rollings

Talley Rollings and Lt. Tuthill, unknown officers on the right.

1960s

By 1960, the Department had grown significantly compared to its staffing in 1950—there were three hundred twenty-three officers compared to one hundred seventy-four. The number of vehicles had nearly doubled to sixty-two compared to thirty-three. The city crime rate had increased as well as evidenced by the number of arrests. In 1950, there had been 25,465 arrests. At the end of 1960, the number for the year was 60,234. Chief Dudley McFadyen had led the Department since 1941, and he had made many improvements in equipment, personnel, and efficiency. In 1961, he retired, and the reins of leadership were passed to Talley Rollings.

K9 Corps

During the summer of 1962, Chief Talley Rollings determined that the Mobile Police Department needed a K9 unit. The military had used dogs for years in the service of the country, and now police departments around the country were developing their own K9 programs. The biggest difference would be the roles the dogs would play. The military dogs were trained to kill, police dogs were trained to search and detain. Chief Rollings stated that the purpose of the new K9 Corps, as it was to be called, was to conduct riot control, search buildings for burglars, ride with the officers on routine patrol, and conduct walking patrols in high-crime areas.

Doctor Robert Hall and his wife donated the first German shepherd dog to the program. The dog was named Scrappy, and he was given Badge #1. The first officer assigned was Officer Frank Terlow. Terlow was a Navy veteran, having served in World War II. He joined the Mobile Police Department on June 19, 1956. The second donated German shepherd was named Buffalo, called Buff, and he was given badge #2. His handler

170

was Officer Samuel "Joeseph" Martin, who joined the Department on July 4, 1957.

A new K9 training facility had opened in New Orleans, Louisiana, and both officers and dogs were sent to it in August 1962. The officers and dogs graduated the fourteen-week training course and returned to Mobile. They were assigned to patrol duties and quickly showed their worth by capturing several burglars. The two officers conducted demonstrations for local business and civic groups which generated much praise and support. The two officers were so successful in their duties that a third officer was added in early 1963.

The third officer was Officer Daniel Goldman who had been hired on February 1, 1962, and his new K9 partner was Sky. With this addition, the arrests rose, and the community was enthralled with the unit. Commendations poured in from citizens, churches, businesses such as Alabama Power, Merchants National Bank, Cunningham and Bounds Law Firm, Cub Scout Packs, The Civitan Club, and even the United States Air Force at Brookley Field. The Lions Club went so far as to send a request to Commissioner Joseph Langan to increase the number of dogs and officers in the unit to ten each.

By March 1963, three additional German shepherds were donated to the Department. Those three were named Rommel, Mark, and Nero. The three officers assigned would be assigned two dogs each.

By the end of the 1963, the unit had become an invaluable part of the Department and new officers would be assigned as needed. Officer Goldman resigned from the Department in December 1963. Officer Terlow resigned in 1967 and became a boat captain in Bayou LaBatre. Officer Martin left the department in 1982.

The K9 Corps eventually became known as the K9 Detail and is currently assigned to the Special Operations Division. The unit is comprised of one sergeant, one corporal and four officers, each with their own assigned K9 partner.

The current MPD K9 unit:
Officer Lane Lowry-K9 Tex, Corporal Joshua Evans-K9 Gunner,
Sergeant Donnel McKean-K9 Hyco,
Officer Blake Russell-K9 Bowie,
Officer Oliver Simpson-K9 Muck, Officer Daniel Hill- K9 Nelly

Late 1960s

In the late 1960s, the Department still struggled to obtain funding and personnel. The League of Women Voters released a pamphlet called "This is Mobile" in 1968, and one of the pages provided information on the police department at that time.

The present Chief [James Robinson, July 1963-December 1970] was appointed by the City Commissioners. Since then, the position has been placed on Civil Service with future Chiefs to be placed by City Commissioners after approval of the Personnel Board. The salary ranges from $1031 to $1176 per month.

The Mobile Police Force has 250 full time, sworn officers, including 184 patrolmen. The qualifications for policeman are: 22 to 35 years of age, high school graduate or equivalent, pass a polygraph exam, pass Civil Service test, pass interview, and have a clean record. The salary ranges from $391 to $533 per month.

There is an 8 hour day, 5 day work week. Compensatory time is allowed for overtime and off duty time spent in court, but due to the department's manpower shortage, this overtime is difficult to pay back. The number of officers in 1968 is 52 short of the number recommended six years before.

There is an annual uniform allowance of $100. Officers furnish guns, shells, uniforms: everything except badge, nightstick, and helmet.

Retirement is at half pay after 20 years at age 55.

There are 5 cadets, 53 school traffic women and 78 civilian personnel.

There is a police station on lower Government Street and one precinct on Gayle Street. The department has a modern communication system-this, working with an around-the-clock patrol system, makes police assistance available immediately in any part of the city and in the police jurisdiction which extends three miles beyond the city limits.

New policemen are given a 6 weeks' training course as well as periodic inservice [sic] training.

The 1967-68 city budget appropriates $2,445,296 for police. A recent survey of 25 cities by the Mobile Police Department showed Mobile 24th in per capita expenditure for police protection.

Riot Squad

In the summer of 1967 public disorder had grown in cities across the country, and it was rightfully believed that these situations would make their way to Mobile. In September, Chief Robinson ordered the creation of three riot squads. The squads were to be used to maintain order, suppress burning, looting, and for crowd control in the event of any civil disorder or natural disaster.

Forty-four officers were selected to fill the three squads. Each squad was comprised of twelve men with a squad leader. Four men were assigned to the tear gas section, one was a platoon commander, one was field platoon commander, and one was assistant field commander, with the remaining officer assigned as the driver of the riot squad bus.

The initial training for the group was conducted at the pistol range and consisted of crowd control, psychological factors involved in mob behavior and riot control formations, and close order drill. Pistols and shotguns were fired extensively. The initial training was conducted one day each week until everyone was fully trained on the new tactics. Afterwards, the training was conducted whenever conditions allowed. The members were allowed to wear a small triangle patch, red in color, trimmed in gold with the letter "R" in gold, on their right shoulder sleeve. At that time, MPD officers only had a shoulder patch on the left sleeve.

Within a year, the new riot squad had been used for the 1968 and 1969 Mardi Gras, Martin Luther King's assassination protests, the school crisis of 1968. and the 1969 Junior Miss Pageant. In that time, the Riot Squad had made over eight hundred arrests with no injuries reported or citizen complaints filed. The officers assigned were paid an additional $25 per month, which led some to call it the Twenty-five Dollar a Month Club.

For the next decade, officers who wished to become members of the Riot Squad would have to fill out an application, pass the interview and the physical testing before being placed on the rolls. If an officer wished to be removed from the squad, he had to submit a letter of resignation to the commander of the unit who would then submit it to the Chief of Police for approval.

On March 25, 1976, the Mobile County Personnel Board approved the recommendation of the Department to abolish the Riot Squad position and the $25-a-month incentive. By this time, the Riot Squad had grown to include fifty-four officers, but it was being disbanded to create the SWAT team. The concept of a "riot control squad" would be revisited thirty-eight years later due to nationwide events.

Quick Reaction Force

In 2014, the need for a group of officers assigned to a riot squad or crowd control team arose. Nationwide, there were anti-police riots breaking out due to an officer-involved shooting in Ferguson Missouri. Mobile had a few protests occur, but nothing like what was happening in cities like St. Louis, Los Angeles, Milwaukee, and other large cities. The potential for violence and riots was increasing, nonetheless. Due to these emerging threats, the Quick Reactionary Force or "QRF" was formed.

The unit was created to manage crowds and preserve peace during demonstrations and civil disturbances. The officers are assigned by the Chief of Police, and required to attend training and any call-out that may arise. Training is conducted quarterly.

The QRF is commanded by a captain with an additional captain assigned as an assistant. It is comprised of two platoons of four squads each. Each platoon has two lieutenants who are in command of two squads. Each squad has one sergeant, one corporal and nine officers. The platoons are filled with personnel who are assigned to patrol shifts one and four or two and three. This allows a platoon complement to be on duty any given day.

Unknown patrol officers, MPD archives

Unknown officer, MPD archives

The 1970s

Police Helicopter

On January 5, 1970, City Commissioner Joe Bailey, who was serving as mayor at the time, along with Commissioners Robert Doyle and Lambert Mims, issued a directive to Chief of Police James Robinson that created a Mobile Police Department Aviation Detachment. The Aviation Detachment would be assigned to the Identification Division and commanded by Captain Wendell Stowe. Officer Paul Beadnell would be assigned to the detachment as Chief Pilot, second in command. Officers James McLaughlin and J.W. Smith would serve as co-pilots.

Commissioner Doyle had earlier approached U.S. Representative Jack Edwards of Mobile for assistance in having a helicopter donated to the Mobile Police Department. At the time, the Federal Government had the Law Enforcement Assistance Administration in place to assist law enforcement agencies with training, funding, and equipment. Part of this program included aviation training at Fort Rucker, Alabama.

Officers Beadnell, McLaughlin, and Smith along with Clarence Williams reported to Fort Rucker for a six-month-training course that would teach and certify the three officers how to fly helicopters. Williams was trained and certified to be the flight mechanic. The cost of the training was $6,500 each and was paid for by the Law Enforcement Assistance Administration. The City of Mobile covered the travel expenses for the four men. In January 1972, the Law Enforcement Assistance Administration cancelled the $440,000 they had been paying for the aviation training program, essentially shutting it down.

U.S. Representative Edwards was able to secure a helicopter for the city, and it was donated in March of 1972. The helicopter was a $75,000 Fairchild-Hiller that would seat four. It had available options such as water tanks that could help extinguish forest fires. Officers Beadnell and Smith traveled to El Paso, Texas, to take possession of the helicopter, and they flew it to Mobile. It was housed in one of the hangars at the now-closed Brookley Air Force Base off of I-10 and Michigan Avenue.

Helicopter at Brookley Field. MPD archives.

The three officers assigned to the Aviation Detachment were only there part-time. Each of them had primary positions on the department. Officers Beadnell and Smith were assigned to the Identification Detail, and Officer McLaughlin was assigned to Traffic Division as a motorcycle officer. Clarence Williams was the only full-time member of the Aviation Detachment, and his role was to keep the helicopter mechanically sound and prep it when a call for service was made.

The U.S. Coast Guard Aviation Training Center in Mobile assisted the officers with their continued training and gave them equipment such as life rafts and other lifesaving supplies for air-sea operations.

The helicopter was used on occasion in 1972 and early 1973. On July 2 and 3, 1972, the helicopter was used to search for a missing boater in the Tensaw River. Mobile County Chief Investigator Tom Dees' boat was found floating near the L and N train tracks at the Tensaw River. It is believed that he was attempting to replace a broken shear pin on the motor when he fell overboard. The helicopter was used in conjunction with the flotilla.

The helicopter was used in the search for missing persons in the Gulf of Mexico, and the officers were responsible for the rescue of a young woman.

On January 7, 1973, the helicopter was used to search Mobile Bay for a small airplane that had been reported missing. On January 6, the small plane was carrying five passengers from Fort Walton, Florida, to Gulfport, Mississippi, when it went down in the bay. Eyewitnesses in Spanish Fort, Alabama, reported seeing the small airplane flying low towards Mobile around 6 pm. It is believed the plane crashed during bad weather as it was trying to make it to Brookley Field. One of the passengers, an eleven-year-old girl, was found deceased, floating in the water near the Middle Bay Lighthouse.

After January 1973, I can find no record of the helicopter being used, though I am sure that it was, at least occasionally. There were some news articles questioning the money being spent on its upkeep and operation. I have been told that the program was shelved, and the helicopter placed into storage due to the annual cost of the maintenance. The last article I have located about the helicopter was in the fall of 1973 regarding a large globe that had been donated to the city. The plans were to showcase this globe at the Civic Center, but the cost to do so was over $20,000, so it was suggested that the globe be stored with the police helicopter at Brookley Field.

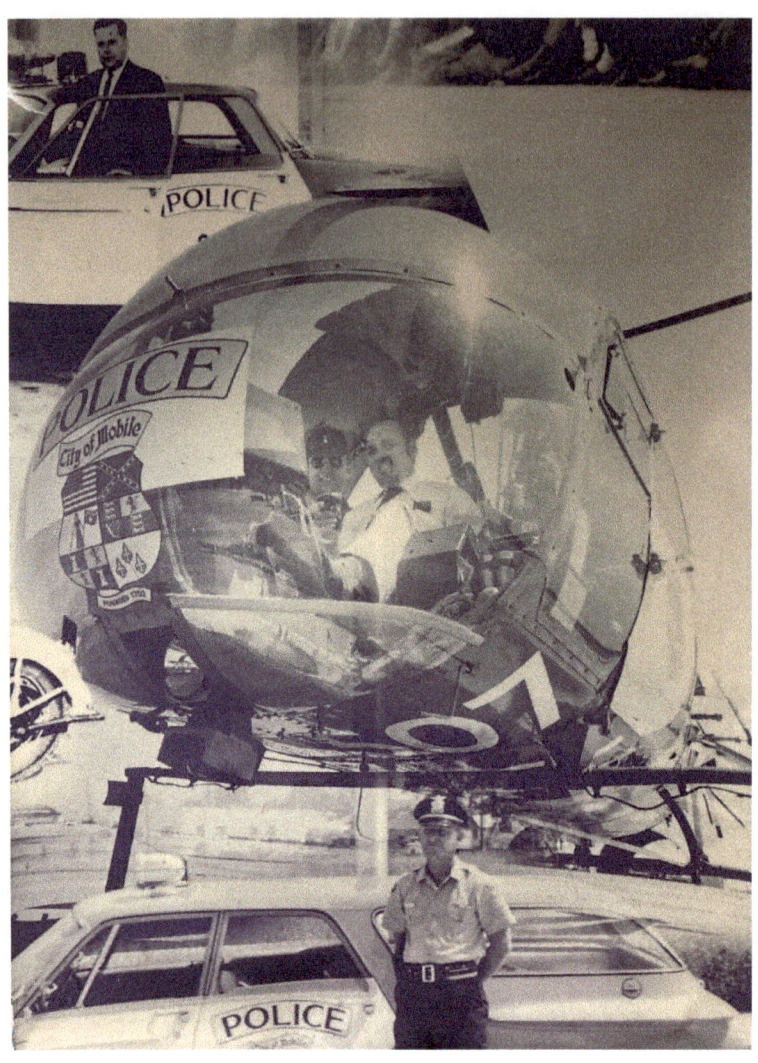

Photograph taken of the wall mural in the old Central Events
Police Precinct Museum.

1970s Traffic Unit

SWAT

For years, police departments across the country dealt with emergency situations or unusual occurrences with selected groups of officers and by bringing in off- duty officers to assist. In the late 1960s, police administrators started to recognize traditional methods were no longer adequate for dealing with the changing patterns of crime and the types of unusual occurrences. The country had seen an increase in instances of sniper activity on college campuses, hijackings, kidnappings, armed robberies, and bombings. To combat this, agencies followed the Los Angeles Police Department model of a Special Weapons and Tactics unit by creating their own SWAT units.

The 1963 Mobile Police Department Emergency Plan specified that there would be a multiple tactical units comprised of men from throughout the Department. There are no records that have been found that indicate when these groups were formed or what additional training they received, but they were called the Commanding Tactical Unit, commanded by Captain J.A. Botta; 2nd Tactical Unit, commanded by Sgt. Elmer Stewart; Third Tactical Unit commanded by Sgt. Alfred Webb; and 4th Squad Tactical Unit (Traffic Division) commanded by Sgt. Michael Conniff.

Each of the four units was comprised of officers and supervisors. Each team had members who would carry specialized equipment such as shotguns, rifles, gas guns, or have a K9. Each team also had assigned vehicles with equipment for the team. Below is the makeup of Squad 4 (Traffic Division).

In order of rank of command:

Sgt. Michael Conniff- In charge
Sgt. Quinton Long- Ass't. Squad Leader
Officer William Thompson- Lead Man

Group A, Squad #4
Sgt. Michael Conniff, Squad Leader
Artlip, Douglas
Lee, Travis (Shotgun)
McGallagher, Henden
Talbott, Clarence
Beadnell, Paul (Rifleman)
Jeslin, Eural (Shotgun)

Group B, Squad #4
Sgt. Quinton Long-Asst. Squad Leader
Thompson, William (Gas Gun)
Gibson, Harry
Price, John
Purvis, James (Shotgun)
Newell, Gus (Shotgun)
Denmark, Verne

Vehicles:
Car #93- Gas Gun, 300 feet Rope, Tear Gas Grenade, Ammunition
Car #94-   "   "   "   "
Car #104 "   "   "   "

The orders further state: All Tactical Unit Officers will carry their special equipment with them in their vehicles. If a situation warrants the mobilization of the Tactical Unit at one point with all equipment, the order can come from Captain Botta or the Chief of Police. Upon such a call, all Tactical Unit Officers will leave their areas and meet where directed.

On September 29, 1974, Chief Riddle sent a group of officers to Quantico, Virginia, to the FBI Academy SWAT training school for a one-week course, concluding on October 4, 1974. The Officers sent were Lieutenant Guyland Glen Hodges, Sergeant Jesse Ollie Robertson, Patrolman Roderick David Roy, Patrolman Roderick Harvington Steade, and Patrolman Phillip Wayne Tipp. After their training, this small group of officers served as the only specially trained weapons unit on the department until early 1976.

Chief Riddle recognized that to be successful, he needed to have additional officers trained on special tactics. He reached out to the United States Marine Corp Training Center Commandant in Mobile to see if they could provide this training. On December 8, 1975, the Commandant of the Marine Corps gave permission to the local Marine Corp Training Center to conduct the training.

Before this could be implemented, Chief Riddle needed to obtain the permission of the three city commissioners. Each of them signed off on the project in February 1976. The Mobile County Personnel Board approved the measure in late March 1976, and on April 6, 1976, the pay-scale for officers selected to SWAT was approved. Twenty-eight officers would make up the SWAT Unit.

The first SWAT Unit was made up of a commander, who would be a lieutenant or higher rank, three team leaders, three squad leaders and twenty-one officers. There were three teams made up of nine members. Each member of the team was trained in every position of the team, and they were able to work and train independently or with the other two teams.

The first organization chart for the Mobile Police Department SWAT Unit was:

Commander		
Team Leader	Team Leader	Team Leader
Squad Leader	Squad Leader	Squad Leader
Marksman (rifle)	Marksman (rifle)	Marksman (rifle)
Marksman (spotter)	Marksman (spotter)	Marksman (spotter)
Automatic Weapons	Automatic Weapons	Automatic Weapons
Shotgunner	Shotgunner	Shotgunner
Gasman	Gasman	Gasman
Reserve	Reserve	Reserve
Reserve	Reserve	Reserve

On April 25, 1979, Chief Riddle issued Special Order 79-30 which stated that effective April 27, 1979, Sergeant Obie Singletary would be the Officer in Charge of the Police Department's Bomb Technician Team. It outlined the requirements for application to the team and the training required. The officers selected would be trained by the Mobile Police Department and then sent to the Hazardous Devices School in Huntsville, Alabama. This was the beginning of the process to create a Bomb Squad. The process would take some time.

On January 10, 1980, Chief Riddle wrote to Commissioner Robert Doyle that to create the Bomb Squad, seven positions on the SWAT team would be eliminated. The Bomb Squad would be attached to SWAT and consist of a senior bomb technician and six bomb technicians. On January 15, 1980, the Personnel Board approved the request to create the Bomb Squad and also approved the request to pay the same $50 incentive to those officers as SWAT members.

On February 6, 1980, Chief Riddle wrote to Commissioner Doyle stating three officers had been certified as Bomb Technicians and should receive the agreed-upon incentives. The remaining four officers were still in training. The first three to be certified were Sergeant Obie Singletary, Police Officer Roy Adams, and Police Officer Otis Richerson. The next two officers to be certified were Police Officer II

Larry Hearn and Police Officer I Benny Twiggs on April 18, 1980. The remaining two positions remained vacant.

The SWAT unit in this configuration was short lived as was the training conducted with the Marine Corps. In the summer of 1980, officers on the Department went on strike. As a form of punishment or retribution, the SWAT team was disbanded for taking part in the strike. On August 23, 1980, the SWAT team ceased to exist. The Bomb Squad was left intact as a standalone unit.

Currently, the Bomb Squad is known as Emergency Ordinance Disposal (EOD.) There are two full-time members, a sergeant and a corporal. Additional officers are assigned in a call-out capacity. All members conduct monthly training.

On December 8, 1980, Captain Robert Larison submitted a request to Chief Riddle to create a new emergency response team that would replace the existing SWAT team. The name SWAT would not be used, and the previous SWAT team members would not be allowed to serve, but the mission and purpose of the unit would remain the same.

The proposal was to staff the new ERT team with one commander, (lieutenant or higher), two team leaders (sergeants only), and ten patrol officers. There were to be two six-man teams. The members would be selected from the patrol division only. The members would be assigned to patrol squads, and their primary duty was patrol and answering calls. Officers selected to the position would be given a one-step pay raise as incentive. They would also be allowed up to sixteen hours a month in overtime for physical and equipment training.

Officers who wanted to join the ERT were required to have served on the department for a minimum of two consecutive years, and they had to apply. The candidate had to obtain a physical examination from a licensed physician. Additionally, they had to pass a one-mile run, wall climbing, rappelling, general calisthenics, and pass the physical standards prescribed by the Civil Service including height and weight to within plus or minus ten pounds.

On February 21, 1981, the Emergency Response Team was created. The first members were:

Lieutenant James Taylor (retired as a lieutenant)
Sergeant Jack Bishop (retired as a sergeant)

Sergeant James Braswell (retired as a major)
Officer Stephen Arthur (retired as a captain)
Officer John Graham (retired as a lieutenant)
Officer Claude Monigan (left the department)
Officer David Smith (retired as a corporal)
Officer David Vaughn (left the department)
Officer Joseph Kennedy (retired as an assistant chief)
Officer Robert Duff (retired as a corporal)
Officer Wayne Toole (left the department)
Officer Glen Brannan (retired as a lieutenant)
Officer Eddie Carr (retired as a sergeant)

On June 19, 1985, a request was made by Lieutenant Steve Scarcliff to create a third Emergency Response Team. The request was denied due to funding.

Between the adoption of the ERT in 1981 and 1985, there had only been one SWAT school training attended by Mobile Police Department personnel. In October 1984, Frank Sullivan, Joseph Kennedy, Stephen Arthur, and William Sekel attended SWAT Training at Valencia Community College. All other members had been trained by previously trained members and on-the-job training.

ERT continued to operate in this form until the end of 1992. Chief Harold Johnson changed the unit's name to Tactical Response Unit (TRU). The officers were taken out of their patrol assignments and placed in TRU as a standalone unit. The unit was given their own office on Dr. Martin Luther King Avenue where they operated for several years until their offices moved to the Western Administrative Complex on Museum Drive. The officers in the unit were placed back into patrol due to personnel shortages in the mid 1990s, but that only lasted for a brief period. The Tactical Response Unit was known as TRU and then the abbreviated form TAC, but officially, it was Tactical Response Unit.

In 2002, the TRU was awarded the Tactical Response Unit Citation for Valorous Actions by the National Tactical Officers Association for their response to a call on October 24, 2001. That call involved a barricaded suspect inside a bar who had shot and wounded three Mobile Police officers, wounded two citizens, and killed another citizen. The team entered the same door that the wounded officers had entered and made a quick search while utilizing diversion tactics. The suspect opened fire, but the officers were able to incapacitate him before any other citizen or officer was wounded or killed. That was the first fatal shooting by a member of the Team during a tactical call in its twenty-five year history. The team members who received the award were: Sergeant Kevin Thompson, Sergeant Jerry Hoven, Corporal Phillip McCrary, Corporal Clay Godwin, Corporal Leon Torbert, Corporal Kevin Rodgers, Officer Will Shaffer, Officer Paul Check, Officer Charles Pharr, Officer Jeffery Woodruff, Officer Timothy Perrin, and Officer Brian Overstreet.

In 2014, Chief James Barber had the name of the unit changed back to SWAT.

SWAT Team, June 1977

First Female Patrol Officer

In 1971, the City of Mobile and the Mobile Police Department were sued by a group of Black police officers for discrimination in promotions and working assignments. As a result of the lawsuit, the Department was under a Federal mandate that prohibited them from discrimination. By the mid-1970s, the women's equal rights movement was well underway, and legislation was being passed that would give women the same rights to employment and pay as men.

It was during this period that the Mobile Police Department hired the first female patrol officers. Prior to this, women had been employed as officers in the department, but their assignments were clerical or traffic related. These women were not allowed to patrol the streets and respond to calls for service.

The Police Department Payroll and Employee Record book of 1944 lists twenty-one women as employees classified as "patrolwoman." The records of these women indicate that they were school crossing guards as they were employed during the months when school was in session. Several of these women were only employed during either January through May or September through December. Their pay was $100 per month.

Bessie Ibsen, born on September 19, 1926, is recognized as the first female police officer. She was hired on May 1, 1962, and she retired on April 23, 1982. It is believed she is the first female hired as a police officer in the State of Alabama, but that is not confirmed. Bessie complained that she was relegated to menial tasks, desk duties, and denied promotional opportunities. She was told promotions were for policemen not policewomen, and she threatened to sue in Federal Court. She was ultimately promoted to sergeant in January 1977, but she was never allowed to patrol or partake in any duties other than the menial jobs, desk duty, and clerical work that she had complained about.

Bessie Ibsen, September 11, 1962.

Bessie Ibsen, PD Martial Arts class, March 11, 1963.

The Manual of Rules and Regulations of the Mobile Police Department, dated June 1964 read as follows: Article VII Criminal Investigation Division, Section 10:

Duties-
POLICEWOMAN,
She shall be subordinate to the Lieutenant, and perform such duties as required of the Criminal Investigator, where applicable.

The rules of the Department clearly defined the role of a female police officer, and it was clear, women would not be treated the same as men on the department.

On January 5, 1976, Linda Sue Mozingo and Sandra J. Martin were hired under the classification of patrolman. They attended a six-week training course at Faulkner State Junior College in Bay Minette, Alabama, and then a one-week course at the Mobile Police Department. Upon completion of this training, the officers were assigned duties in the Department.

It should be noted that the administration, including Mayor Doyle, weren't enthusiastic about the hires. As noted in a "Mobile Register" article from January 1, 1976, Mayor Doyle was quoted as saying, "We wanted to hire some females in the police department because that's what we've got to do." Despite this, Linda Mozingo made statements that she didn't feel shunned by the officers or supervisors she worked with. By November 1976, an additional nine women had filed applications with the department.

Linda Mozingo was assigned to the Docket room after her initial training and remained there until April 1976 when she was transferred to a patrol squad. Sandra Martin's employment record could not be located other than when she resigned from the department on October 8, 1978.

The badges officers Mozingo and Martin were issued had the word "Patrolman" on them, as that was the Personnel Board classification for the job. On March 1, 1977, that classification was changed to "Police Officer.". The badges, however, were not changed until the mid-1980s.

Linda Mozingo was featured in several news articles that told of her activities while at work on the department. She made burglary arrests, robbery arrests, and investigated accidents. She did write and conduct the initial investigation into a juvenile sexual assault case that drew attention to the area. Her work led to the arrest of David Jose, who was stationed at the Pensacola Naval Air Station. He was ultimately charged with a string of four child molestation cases that occurred in Mobile between November 1976 and January 1977.

In January 1982, the Department created a new Sex Crimes Unit, and Linda was one of the first three officers assigned. Clearly her work ethic excelled. Later that year, in May, she was promoted to Sergeant. During the summer of

1982, she attended the FBI National Academy at Quantico, Virginia. She graduated with Class 129 that summer. Upon her return from the National Academy, she was transferred to the Patrol Division where she became the first female patrol sergeant in the history of the Mobile Police Department.

Officer Linda Mozingo, Sgt. Tommy Hart, Lester Hargrove, Officer Dorothy Smith far right, others unknown.

Newly promoted Sergeant Linda Mozingo, May 20, 1982.

Linda Mozingo blazed a trail for future female officers and set a high standard for them. By March 1986, there were seventeen women on the Department. Linda resigned from the Department on January 1, 1988, and moved from the area.

1980s

The Strike

In 1979, city employees were becoming increasingly unhappy with the City Commissioners and their failure to provide pay increases and improved benefits. At the time, the Commissioners were Robert Doyle, Mayor and Public Safety; Gary Greenough, Finance; and Lambert Mims, Public Works. Merit raises or cost-of-living raises had not been given in several years, and many city employees had to take on second or third jobs to make ends meet. The police department did not provide uniforms or equipment to the officers. The individual officer was required to purchase his uniform and equipment. The current rate of pay did not provide what many considered a living wage.

The Mobile County Law Enforcement Association, MCLEA, was the "union" that represented law enforcement officers in Mobile County. There were several members in the union from agencies within Mobile County, but the vast majority of the MCLEA members were Mobile Police Officers. The MCLEA began sending requests for pay raises and improved benefits to the City Commissioners. The Mobile Fire Department employees union did the same. One of the complaints of the employees was that when they were hired, they were told that the City would provide them with a five percent merit raise each year for employees in good standing. Those raises had not been given in three years. (When I was hired in 1992, I was told the same thing during the hiring process. And just like in 1979, it was untrue).

For nearly a year-and-a-half, the city employees lobbied the Commissioners to improve their pay and benefits. For that entire time, the Commissioners provided a deaf ear and excuses as to why they could not implement pay raises. The Commissioners or the City's Finance Director did meet with the groups on four occasions in 1979. But these meetings were considered a waste of time by the employees because all they were given were excuses as to why the City couldn't help them.

By May of 1980, several employee unions or groups had provided the Commissioners with their requests. The most common request from the various groups was to be given a twenty percent cost-of-living increase. The request was to have this implemented either all at one time or in increments within a one-year period. The Commissioners balked. Communications between the employees and the Commissioners continued into July.

On July 14, 1980, the Commissioners sent a letter to all city employees that stated the Commission had reviewed the proposals made during May and June of that year. They stated the annual cost to the city to implement raises would be approximately $7,350,000. For the other requests, they stated "some of the proposals are reasonable" and that the city would be willing to favorably address them, but they did not specify which requests or when they would take action on them. They concluded the letter stating that they couldn't specify what type of raise or when one could be given but they would strive to reduce operating costs. The city employees considered the letter as just word play and political speak to cover their inaction.

After the letter was received on the 14th, the firefighters began striking. Four hundred twenty firefighters walked out. The police officers and MCLEA called for strike meeting to be held on Wednesday, July 16, at 1200 hours. They met at the Insulators Local 55 at 908 Butler Drive to vote on whether they would join the strike. The vote was a resounding yes. It was agreed that the strike would begin that day during shift change between 1400 and 1500 hours. The MCLEA was quoted as saying two hundred fifty would strike, but those numbers probably included the dispatchers who also voted to strike with the officers. The Police Benevolent Association, which was primarily a Black police officer organization, stated that their thirty members would not join the strike because the organization had a prohibition against striking in its by-laws. By July 19 though, several of the Black officers had joined the striking officers.

That day, after the Department became aware of the strike, Chief Donal Riddle issued a Departmental Special Order, number S.O. 80-33. The order stated to all personnel that effective immediately, all off days and vacation were cancelled. Employees were directed to contact their supervisors for assignments and hours. It was to remain in effect until otherwise notified by the Chief's office.

It has been estimated that about half of the oncoming afternoon shift on July 16 did not show up for work. Over the next several days, those numbers would increase. To provide coverage for the city, twelve-hour shifts were implemented, and detectives, supervisors, and traffic officers were reassigned to answering calls and patrolling the city. Non-priority calls were not answered, and the public was told that if they had petty theft cases to report, to mail the information into the department. Alabama Governor Fob James activated the Alabama National Guard and sent one hundred forty of them to Mobile. Their primary function was to assist in fighting fires and protecting empty fire stations. They were not used for law enforcement purposes.

The City Commissioners began meeting with the employee unions in an effort to end the strikes. Their efforts appear to have been in bad faith. On July 19, the Commissioners issued a notice to all City of Mobile Police Officers that they would implement a five percent merit raise for "those entitled" effective the next pay period and a blanket five percent raise. The catch was the five percent merit raise would not be given to any officer who had been absent from post without leave. Additionally, the other proposals by employees were not addressed but would be negotiated in the future.

The Commissioners created a committee to meet with the various union representatives. The committee was comprised of Pierre Pelham a former state legislator; William Weaver, Mobile College President; local banker Paul Sheldon, Sonny Niehart with the Building Trade Council, and former City Commissioner Arthur Outlaw. The MCLEA met with them one time, and nothing came of it. After the meeting, MCLEA attorney John Grow stated they would not meet with the committee again. There was no point in meeting with an entity that had no authority to enact changes.

The striking officers, firefighters, dispatchers, wives, and family members picketed at various locations in the city. They had a picket line at the patrol division building at 1251 Virginia Street, the Public Works Department on Gayle Street, the Police Headquarters, and City Hall. The Public Works employees did not go out on strike, but they refused to cross the picket lines. Garbage would not be picked up throughout the city. The public was told that collection bins for garbage would be placed at various parks throughout the city, but it was requested that they only dropped off items that would rot if not disposed of. Other city services were impacted as well. The Animal Shelter employees would not cross the picket lines.

The City filed for injunctions against the strikers, and Judge Braxton Kittrell issued an order to end the strike and to remove the pickets from in front of the Public Works facility. On the 18th, the firefighters left the location, but the police department continued to picket.

Police pickets were placed at the Mobile Transit Authority at 570 Beauregard Street over the weekend of the 19th and 20th, which led to the MTA requesting an emergency injunction or temporary restraining order be issued by the court. Judge Kittrell denied their request. The strike continued.

On July 19, Sergeant R. Roy called a meeting with the on-duty shift at the request of Captain Milne. They met in the Woolco Shopping Center at Springhill and I65 at 0305 hours. It was reported that Captain Milne told the officers that he would meet them at the Virginia Street Precinct, outside the picket lines to check the officers off and that he would have their cars driven into the property so the officer would not have to. It was also reported that he told the group "if you have any balls, you'll walk, and if you don't, you'll stay." Only one officer walked.

Talks between the unions and the Commissioners continued but were not productive. They would not budge on the issue of the merit raise excluding the striking workers, and they would not address the proposals of the union. The situation was deteriorating to the point that the Commander of the National Guard that was deployed in the city met with the Commissioners in an effort to get them to resolve the issue. It was reported, though some say incorrectly, that the Commander threatened to pull the National Guard out of the City. It was later reported that he told the Commissioners that he could not keep the Guard there indefinitely.

The MCLEA created a document that laid out their proposals with signature lines for their representatives and the Commissioners to sign upon agreement. The document is as follows:

AGREEMENT

This Agreement made and entered into on this _____ day of July 1980, by and between the MOBILE COUNTY LAW ENFORCEMENT ASSOCIATION, on behalf of all employees of the Mobile Police Department, and the CITY OF MOBILE, a Municipal corporation, by and through its duly elected Commissioners, in an effort to resolve existing disputes between the parties do hereby covenant and agree with each other as follows:

1. The parties agree that there is to be complete and total amnesty for any and all persons resulting from any failure to report to work, picketing, or other activities arising from the work stoppage heretofore entered into by employees of the Mobile Police Department. This amnesty extends to any and all captains, lieutenants, sargents (sic), patrolmen, probationary employees and Ceta employees of the Mobile Police Department. Attached hereto and made a part hereof as Exhibit A is a list of the names of police officers who participated in the work stoppage heretofore in affect by the employees of the Mobile City Police Department. This list is not meant to be nor do the parties consider it as being all inclusive of those employees covered by the foregoing amnesty clause.

2. Effective upon signing of this Agreement the parties agree that there will be a ten (10%) pay increase across the board for each employee of the Mobile Police Department. The parties further agree that the City of Mobile will pay the employee's share of the FICA

taxes, said payment by the City to be effective immediately.

3. The City of Mobile agrees that it will institute additional insurance coverage to cover the family of the employees of the Mobile City Police Department for dental and eye coverage. Said dental and eye coverage is to be negotiated and to be approved by the Mobile County Law Enforcement Association.

4. The City of Mobile agrees that they will establish a uniform depository for all shoes, uniforms and other equipment used by the employees of the Mobile City Police Department.

5. The City of Mobile further agrees that it will institute a retirement plan which provides vested benefits to the employees of the Mobile City Police Department after five (5) years for any job related or non-job related medical condition which results in total medical disability. Said retirement plan is to be subject to the approval of the Mobile County Law Enforcement Association.

6. The City of Mobile agrees that is [sic] will institute a vacation plan similar to the plan provided for the postal employees of the United States Government. The City of Mobile further agrees that it will institute a sick leave policy without penalty. Both vacation and sick leave plans are subject to the approval of the Mobile County Law Enforcement Association.

7. The City of Mobile further agrees that it will institute a program to assure the employees of the Mobile City Police Department that there will be a complete cessation of the harassment policies that have been the

subject of great dissatisfaction of all employees of the Mobile Police Department.

8. The City of Mobile agrees that there will be no deduction from the wages of any of the employees mentioned in Paragraph 1, hereof, and specifically listed on Exhibit A hereof due to any work stoppage in which the employees have heretofore engaged.

9. The City of Mobile agrees that all merit increases due to employees of the Mobile City Police Department will be paid on the date that each employee is entitled to a merit increase.

10. The City of Mobile agrees that there will be established a safety committee, consisting of two patrolmen, one sargent [sic], and one police operator to approve all equipment purchases made by the City of Mobile which are used for patrol purposes, including but not limited to, all vehicles, police communications, weapons, and ammunition.

This agreement which is entered into this date is made with the understanding that the parties hereto have entered same with the expectation of full and fair dealings by the parties hereto and for the purpose of resolving the grievances of the employees of the Mobile City Department.

MOBILE COUNTY LAW ENFORCEMENT   CITY OF MOBILE
ASSOCIATION

Exhibit A is not included here. It contains the names of 157 officers who engaged in the strike.

On July 21, the Commissioners issued their response to the proposal. It is as follows:

July 21, 1980

Please address reply to   P.O. Box 1827
                            Mobile, Ala. 36633

In Response to Your Proposals Submitted
By Your Committee July 21, 1980

_____

The following is a response to the problems that have arisen in the Mobile Police Department.

Several are matters that could have been addressed at the Departmental level. Hopefully, in the future, these problems can be resolved before reaching the Board of Commissioners.

1. In regards to the problems within the Department and in particular the patrol division, the Public Safety Commissioner will develop a concept to deal with these problems with the input from the patrolmen, the supervisors, and the staff. This process will begin within thirty (30) days.

2. Concerning amnesty, the City Commission will not grant full and complete amnesty. Those employees who were AWOL will not be paid for those days absent and further will be disciplined under the rules and regulations of the Personnel Board. It will be the recommendation of the Board of Commissioners that those employees actively engaged in strike activities be suspended one (1) day for every day on strike.

3. The Commission agrees to appoint Sgt. Wilber Williams to the insurance committee of the City of Mobile, allowing his input on upcoming alternate insurance discussions.

4. The Commission favors the concept of an expanded equipment depository to include flashlights, nightsticks, and shoes, but must determine the financial impact of these additions. Once determined, and within fiscal limits, these additions will be made, if necessary, within a phased program. Uniforms for communications workers will be added as soon as practical.

5.   In regards to a revised vacation plan and the related funeral leave question, we will have the Finance Department, along with key department heads, analyze the impact on the budget and on the availability of manpower.

6.   The question of merit increases has already been addressed.

7.   The Public Safety Commissioner will submit information concerning the structure and makeup of a "Safety Board" to the City Commission at the earliest possible date. The Commission will form such a Board.

8.   Legitimate sick leave should not affect the service ratings of employees, however, the rating form needs to be studied in order to determine how this can be accomplished.

9.   We realize that all new officers need time on the beat with experienced officers and the Commission is in favor of this. However, the allocation of manpower is left to the discretion of supervisory personnel.

10. The City Commission has authorized a 5% merit increase for those employees eligible, plus a 5% blanket raise already in effect. In addition, a 5% blanket raise is committed for April 1, 1981. This $4.1 million package is in our opinion very generous and is all that the budget can stand.

11. We agree to appoint a member of the MPD of the rank of Sgt. or below to the Pension Board, State Law permitting.

Sincerely,
Robert B. Doyle (signature)
Mayor
Lambert C. Mims (signature)
Commissioner
Gary A. Greenough (signature)
Commissioner

The officers rejected the offer of a merit raise without assurances that the striking employees would be eligible to receive it. They also thought that blanket cost-of-living raises were a better option because everyone would receive the raises. If it was a merit raise, an estimated six percent of employees would be ineligible for the raise due to being on probation because they were newly hired or promoted.

By July 22, the Commissioners refused to meet with the MCLEA until the police pickets were removed from the front of Public Works. The Public Works employees were still honoring the picket line and refusing to cross. That afternoon, the Commissioners issued a press release that laid out their position, and it contained not-so-veiled threats of punishment for those employees participating in the strike. They stated that they were bound to this by the rules and regulations of the Personnel Board. In response, on the 22nd, the Personnel Board issued a statement that they would grant full amnesty to anyone who participated in the strike. The Commissioners voiced their opposition to that.

Also on the 22nd, Aetna Life and Casualty Company, the insurance carrier for the City of Mobile employees, issued a letter to the City indicating that they would be terminating coverage for any employee who engaged in a cessation of work as they deemed that to be a termination of employment. That information was passed on to all department heads by the Commission on the 23rd.

On the 23rd, there appeared to be some movement towards a resolution and both the firefighters and police officers were indicating that they would end the strikes and return to duty. The Personnel Board Director had indicated that full amnesty would be granted, and the officers voted to return to duty on the 24th at 1430. When Personnel Board members refused to meet so they could ratify the amnesty deal, the officers continued their strike.

On the 24th, an agreement was reached that would not include amnesty but would provide for lenient punishments for the employees who had engaged in the strike. The punishment would be a one-day suspension for each day that the employee was absent without leave. The firefighters agreed and returned to duty on the morning of the 25th. The police officers agreed as well, and they returned to duty on the 25th at 1430.

The City Commissioners started sending out notices of suspensions by August 20, 1980. Because of the number of police and firefighters who were subject to suspension, they could not suspend everyone at once. The supervisors were to schedule the suspension times in a manner that would not hamper operations. There continued to be disagreements and arguments about the manner in which the discipline was to be handled. The employees, by right, had to be provided a pre-disciplinary hearing. The City's position was that a hearing for all employees would be held at once. The employees wanted individual hearings, and they hired an attorney to represent them. The debate continued well into the fall. In the third week of October, the Personnel Board heard from John Grow, the attorney representing one hundred seventy police officers that the Board was violating the employees' rights by not granting them individual hearings. He stated that despite the hardship of holding so many hearings, it was not a justification for violating their due process rights. He also argued that by the rules and regulations, the employees must have been notified of their suspension within thirty days of the offenses charged.

In the end, the officers were dealt their suspensions. One day for each day they were AWOL. But the lasting effects of the strike cannot be ignored. The officers and firefighters had tried for nearly two years to get the City Commissioners to hear them, to give them a living wage, and to provide benefits. For those nearly two years the City Commissioners refused to take care of the employees. The men and women who walked out were forced into that action by the Commissioners. Speaking with some of the officers who were involved in the strike, they all indicate that they didn't want it to come to that point. They didn't want to harm any citizens, but they were left with no other options other than strike or give up their careers. The men and women currently working on the Mobile Police Department and Mobile Fire Rescue continue to reap the benefits that were brought forth through the efforts of the striking employees.

It should also be noted that in December 1984, Commissioner Gary Greenough was charged and convicted in fourteen cases in Federal Court which stemmed from him conducting schemes and skimming money from the Auditorium (now the Civic Center) and lining his and his friends' pockets. He was sentenced to twenty-five years in the Federal Penitentiary. He appealed, but it was denied. He did gain an early release from prison, and he passed away in Mobile on March 28, 2024.

Group Photos from the 1980s

1982 Police Picnic

1983 Squad

1983 Squad

1983 Squad

1985 Honor Guard

Alabama Police Olympics Softball Team
1989 Gold Medal Winners

1990s

Harold Johnson

In December 1989, Harold Johnson was appointed Chief of Police and became the first Black man to be appointed Chief in the Mobile Police Department's history. This appointment was controversial as could be expected, but not necessarily because of his race, though that most assuredly was an issue with some. The overwhelming factor was, he was an outsider.

Harold Johnson came from Ecorse, Michigan, a small suburb outside of Detroit, Michigan, where he had been the police chief since 1988. Prior to that, he had worked for several years with the Detroit Police Department, and for a time, he was the Public Safety Director of Highland Park, Michigan. He was well-educated, well-trained, and a member of several law enforcement organizations. He did have flaws as well, and being an outsider, those flaws rubbed some a lot worse than if he had been promoted from the ranks.

With the challenges facing him, he made some major missteps when he first arrived. Though most likely not intentional and probably from a cultural difference of being from the north where things are done differently than in the deep south. These missteps cost him buy-in from the officers. One of the biggest missteps with the troops was when meeting a group of officers, he told them that if they didn't do the job correctly, "he would starve their babies." As it could be surmised, this did not go over too well with anyone. Johnson later admitted he had made mistakes and worded things improperly for the audience. What he was trying to say was if officers didn't do their jobs to the standards expected they would face disciplinary action. That action could be a suspension or termination, and both would impact their income.

The controversies lingered for his entire tenure and included conflicts with the city council. His excessive spending, promoting officers that were less qualified than others, taking AM/FM radios out of patrol cars while outfitting himself with a loaded, brand-new car every year were a few of the morale killers he was directly responsible for. Officers found creative ways to "rebel" or "make a stand" against Chief Johnson and his allies. There began to circulate around the department, poems and cartoons. These did improve morale among the troops and rubbed Johnson nearly raw. For several years, the poet would leave his prose for the officers to enjoy. The poems were even addressed in the local media. Johnson downplayed them to the media, but the department knew just how badly he wanted the head of the officer responsible.

He was eccentric, arrogant, and some would say, a blowhard. If you look at individual acts, it would be easy to agree with those assessments. He claimed to have direct contact with the President of the United States. He claimed NASA was working with him, and a Mobile Police Officer would be put into space on one of the missions. That space statement was made to my police academy class in 1992. His resumé and verbal history were called into question, as things just didn't add up. But, looking through the lens of time, it is easy to see that both sides of this conflict were both right and wrong. Neither side would budge, so nothing was ever settled with the morale problems.

To understand where the Department is today, we have to see where it was before Harold Johnson was appointed. The

Mobile Police Department was in turmoil in the late 1980s. There were cliques and loyalties to different political factions. Sheriff Tom Purvis stated in a newspaper article from 1992 that the Mobile Police Department was "out of control." This is the department that Johnson took command of. Then-Mayor Mike Dow stated that he wanted to hire someone from outside the department because there were so many factions and cliques within the department that no one trusted anyone to take over and run the department effectively.

In the mid-1980s, the City of Mobile form of government went from a three-person commission where the "mayor" rotated, to a mayor and council model. Arthur Outlaw was the first mayor under this new system, and he was up for re-election in 1989. Mike Dow ran against him and was elected on September 12, 1989. He was sworn in on October 2, 1989. Before Dow was sworn in, he made the statement that he was going to replace the current Chief of Police, Billy Mingus. Mingus announced that he would retire effective November 4, 1989.

Dow initially stated that he would run the police department while the search for a chief was conducted, but on December 1, 1989, he appointed Captain James Orso to the position of Interim Chief.

On December 9, 1989, Dow met with Ruben Greenburg, the Chief of Police in Charleston, South Carolina. Greenburg had made a name for himself with his community policing policies and the reduction of crime in Charleston. Greenburg was offered the chief of police position, but he was happy in Charleston. He did agree to take a six-month leave of absence and come to Mobile to help with the transition.

On December 27, 1989, Harold Johnson was named Chief. On January 28, 1990, Greenburg was sworn in as the Public Safety Director, and Johnson was sworn in as Chief of Police. Greenburg would remain in the position through June of that year.

Changes swept through the department fairly quickly after Johnson and Greenburg were installed. Additional funding for officers and equipment was secured from the City Council. Federal grant money was obtained to hire officers to work in the housing projects. Headquarters was moved from 51

Government Street to its current location at 2460 Government Boulevard in January 1991.

New units were conceived and formed under the leadership of Harold Johnson.

The Jaguars

The Jaguar Unit was formed in March 1990 by Public Safety Director Reuben Greenberg. They were primarily used in high crime areas, and their focus was on street-level criminal activity. They were instrumental in removing drugs and weapons from the open-air drug markets in certain high-crime neighborhoods. The officers were assigned to ride two-man cars and were always "salt and pepper," meaning a white officer and a black officer. They disbanded around 2014.

Jaguar Patrol Car, 1992

The Rangers

The Ranger Unit was formed in 1990 and was tasked with patrolling the housing projects and embracing the community-oriented policing model that was taking over departments throughout the country at the time. A new "mini precinct" was installed in the Happy Hills Housing Projects in February 1990. The Rangers were given Honda Elite scooters and Suzuki Samurai Jeep-type vehicles to supplement their patrol vehicles.

Rangers, Suzuki Samurai patrol vehicle, 1992

The unit had between five and eight officers on duty for each shift. They worked in all of the housing projects. It should be noted that the Happy Hills Projects were so notoriously violent that officers would not patrol the areas prior to the Rangers taking over, and when officers responded to the scene of any call for service there, they had at least two officers. The Orange Grove, RV Taylor, Birdville, and Roger Williams projects weren't much better in the late 80s and early 90s. The Ranger Unit disbanded in 2016.

Rangers, Honda Elite Scooters, Housing Projects, 1992.

Mounted Unit

The Mounted Unit was formed in 1991. This was the first mounted horse unit in the area in the modern era of policing. There had been a mounted detail on the Department as late as 1915. We have documents that describe the operating costs of having horses on the Department dating to the late 1890s. One of the only photographs that I have found of a mounted rider from that era is from 1913 when President Woodrow Wilson came to Mobile and delivered his Foreign Policy Address, stating the United States would not expand any further by conquest. The photograph is reproduced from the original negative in our archives. It shows Mobile Police Officer Joe Gable on horseback behind the President's car.

President Woodrow Wilson, October 1913.
Officer Joe Gable on horseback.

The idea of a new Mounted Unit was developed under the leadership of Public Safety Director Reuben Greenberg and adopted by Chief Johnson. Sergeant Jack Dove and the Mobile Housing Board wrote a grant proposal that was submitted to the U.S. Department of Housing and Urban Development. The city was granted $200,000 in funding to start the unit, and the funding was continued through 1994. This money was to be used to purchase horses and equipment and to build a facility for the unit as well as pay for nine mounted officers and a stable manager. The barn was built behind the Training Academy at 1251 Virginia Street. The Mounted Unit fell under the Special Operations Division until 2011 when it was moved under the command of the Central Events Commander.

Their primary mission was to patrol the projects on horseback and to engage in community relations. They excelled in bridging the gap between the public and the police department.

Sergeant Eddie Carr led the unit from almost the beginning. He was instrumental in bringing in quality instructors to train the new officers and horses. Sergeant Carr attended training schools to become a certified mounted instructor and soon thereafter, had members of the team trained as instructors as well. He entered the unit in regional police mounted competitions and brought home many trophies and accolades.

Sergeant Eddie Carr, center, Cpl. Richard Bettner, left,
Lt. Bill Rowland, right at the Dauphin Island Mardi Gras Parade
February 2014.

Sergeant Eddie Carr on Apache at Dauphin Island 2014

Their mission took on the added responsibility of patrolling downtown at night on the weekends alongside the Central Events Unit. Sergeant Carr started a civilian auxiliary mounted unit that assisted with patrol duties, training, and fundraising for the unit. This auxiliary unit was comprised of twenty and up to twenty-five civilians who volunteered their time to assist the sworn officers in their duties. The requirements for the auxiliary were that the rider would provide their own horse and trailer, be available to ride at least four hours per month on patrol, and attend training events. The members of the auxiliary were required to pass the same training standards as the sworn officers. The Department provided the auxiliary members with uniform shirts, jackets, bulletproof vests, and jackets. They were unarmed at all times. The auxiliary was so popular, they had members from across lower Alabama, the Pensacola area, Auburn, and as far away as Cumming, Georgia. Kris Sievenpiper drove from north Georgia to Mobile every month to assist with patrols for nearly twenty years.

Auxiliary Member Kris Sievenpiper and Maxie at Mardi Gras

The Mounted Unit started a mounted school for Mardi Gras that has attracted law enforcement participants from around the country as well as from Canada and Germany. Instructors for the Mardi Gras School included renowned mounted instructors such as George Survillo, who commanded the Boston Police Department Mounted Unit during high-profile events such as the Democratic National Convention, the Boston Red Sox World Series riots that broke out near Fenway Park, as well as all Red Sox, Celtics, and Patriots sporting events. He has trained numerous mounted units in the New England area and in Mississippi. The unit brought in John Daziel, a retired London Metropolitan Police Mounted Supervisor, to the school for several years. John also trained the Saudi Arabia military on mounted operations, and he was given the rank of Major by their military. Another instructor was Bill "Feather" Richie, who conducts mounted sensory clinics around the country and as far away as Israel. Several of the Mobile mounted officers have received instructor certification from Bill Richie's clinics.

Christmas Patrol on Dauphin Street 2015
Lt. Billie Rowland, Sgt. Jason Henson, Ofc. Jason Martin, Ofc Josh Hart, Cpl. Richard Bettner

The Mounted School participants from law enforcement agencies are given the opportunity to patrol the Mardi Gras events downtown upon satisfactorily demonstrating their abilities during the school. In 2017, the largest school took place with seventy-five participants. On Mardi Gras Day that year, a total of sixty-two horses were deployed downtown for the festivities.

After the initial purchase of horses, the unit relied on donated horses for replacements. Over time, it became clear that donated stock was not going to adequately provide for the demands of the job. One officer on the unit was allowed to use his personal horse for a few years. In 2013, the donated horses were wearing out, and the Department was unable to find quality replacements. I requested permission to purchase a horse and was told that there was no funding available. I told the Chief that I would purchase a horse for the city to use, but it would be my horse and when I left, the horse would come with me. It was agreed that the City would pay for the feeding, shoeing, and medical needs of the horse while being used for mounted work. I purchased a buckskin Percheron Quarter Horse cross and named him Jameson. He was my primary mount until my departure from command of the unit in June 2017.

Jameson and Lt. Billie Rowland on Dauphin Island 2014

We obtained a donated Belgian, named Murphy and another draft cross horse named Epona. These draft crosses proved to be what the unit needed, and in 2015, the Department agreed to purchase additional horses. We bought draft crosses from the Angola Prison Horse Farm in Louisiana. Those horses beefed up our herd and made a huge impact in our patrol duties downtown.

In April 2024, the City purchased a house, barn, outbuildings, and twenty-five acres in Grand Bay, Alabama, for the Mounted Unit. The old facility was in need of replacement, and it had been discovered that the facility had been built on an old cemetery, so it was decided to rebuild in another location. New construction costs had risen so much that they proved to exceed the anticipated budget. The purchase of the existing horse farm in Grand Bay solved the economic problem. The only real issue with this new facility is the distance from the primary patrol area downtown. It would take an extra fifteen to twenty minutes to drive from the barn to downtown. The advantages of a better facility and double the pasture outweighed the negative of a longer drive. The unit was fully moved into the new facility by September 2024.

Central Events

The Central Events Unit was formed in December 1992, with me, Gwen Mosely, and John Sylvester as the first officers. Chief Harold Johnson met with us and gave us our mandate. The downtown area was being redeveloped and reimagined with Mayor Dow's "String of Pearls" project. We would be assigned to a small geographic area of downtown and tasked with cleaning it up. The area we were initially assigned was bordered on the east by Royal Street, the north by St. Louis Street, the west by Franklin Street and the south by Church Street. It wasn't long before we were covering the whole of the Henry Aaron Loop.

We worked Tuesday through Saturday, 1000 to 1800 hours. We were under the direct supervision of Precinct 1 Captain Lester Hargrove. When we first started the unit, we didn't even have a patrol car. We met at Precinct 1 for roll call and then drove our personal vehicles to the downtown area. If an arrest was made, the beat car would come and transport. It didn't take long for them to realize we would need our own vehicle.

On our first day downtown, we observed transvestites and prostitutes turning tricks in the gazebo of Bienville Square during the lunch hour. Arrests were plentiful. Downtown was the Wild West in those days as it hadn't been strictly patrolled or enforced in quite some time. During the first six months of 1993, there were fifty-two reported robberies in the downtown area. Most of these were robberies to individuals. Downtown had its share of homicides and other violent crimes as well. Dr. Patterson, an abortion doctor, was murdered in the parking lot just behind the X-rated movie theater on Dauphin Street in 1993. There was speculation that he was murdered because of his profession, because of recent murders in the country involving abortion doctors. It turned out, it was just a robbery gone bad.

Officer Billie Rowland in the Cushman car 1993.

We were finally given a patrol car and a three-wheeled Cushman car that had been used years earlier by the meter maids. We also were given access to the Honda Elite motor scooters. The Ranger Unit was using these scooters in the housing projects, and we were given one for our use downtown. It came in handy as it was a great way to get through traffic and parking lots, but as I found out in the summer of 1993, they were dangerous.

In July of 1993, in the early morning, I was riding the scooter east on Dauphin Street approaching Joachim. Suddenly, I saw a car being driven by an elderly male run the red light on Joachim. There was no time to avoid the collision, and I woke in the emergency room at Springhill Hospital. I received no long-lasting injuries, but the scooters were taken from inventory. My accident was the last of several that had occurred with these small vehicles.

Additional officers were added to the unit, and we were moved from the First Precinct to a new office at the Convention Center in 1995. The office was located on the ground floor by the parking garage. It was nice to have an office and additional personnel downtown, but the hours spent at work increased. It was soon discovered that the CSX train stopped several times a day, blocking the entrance/exit of the Convention Center parking lot. These blockages could be as long as thirty or forty minutes. If you didn't time it right, you would not be able to get in or out of the parking area. Many shifts were extended due to the train. With the new officers, Central Events officers now patrolled on a day shift and a night shift, seven days a week.

First Central Events patrol car 1993.

The bars and restaurants were quickly opening along Dauphin Street. In 1992, there were only a couple of bars on Dauphin Street. Hayley's, Vincent Van Go-Go, and GT Henry's were the main bars, and the only restaurants open at night on Dauphin were Wintzell's and Derry's Café. With the "String of Pearls," came an abundance of bars and restaurants. The first to open was Grand Central. The crowds flocked downtown in droves, filling the bars and streets. Events were added to the area, Bay Fest in the fall, Kaleidoscope Fest in the spring, and bars were bringing in bands for weekly concerts. It was an exciting time to be a police officer downtown.

In March 1996, several of the downtown businesses banded together and purchased four Cannondale mountain bikes for the officers in Central Events. These bikes were outfitted with blue lights and sirens and saddlebags to carry paperwork. The bikes turned out to be of great use to the unit and made patrolling the parking lots and outskirts of the area easier and more effective. The first four officers assigned to the bike detail were Troy Bookout, Doug Parmenter, Joseph

Sampson, and Laura Bennett. Eventually, the project proved so successful that an additional eight bikes were purchased.

The next new mode of transportation and patrolling was the Segway. It was a fun tool to use, but it was dangerous and not very practical. You could speed down the street, through parking lots and along sidewalks, but if you hit any pothole or got into the grass in the parks, it became unstable, and you often found yourself on the ground. Several injuries and a broken leg were documented due to their use. The second-generation Segway had better, larger wheels that made it easier to traverse the parks and even the occasional tree root, but they were still more a PR tool than a useful, tactical patrol vehicle. Once you made an arrest or engaged a suspect, the Segway was more hinderance that useful. But they were great fun during Mardi Gras and other large events. The city bought us a golf cart to use as well. That still comes in handy during events such as Mardi Gras or Beer Fest.

On March 15, 1997, things changed downtown. Robert Ellingwood was walking east of Dauphin, approaching Claiborne Street when he was approached by two men. One asked for a cigarette and then pulled a gun. Ellingwood ran, but the suspect fired in his direction, striking him twice in the back. Ellingwood ran another thirty-five feet and collapsed. I was standing at the corner of Dauphin Street and Jackson Street and never heard the shot over the crowd and bar noise. I saw the crowd running in my direction yelling about the shooting. As I got to Ellingwood, I tried to reassure him, but I could see the life go out of his eyes. I went to USA Medical Center and was in the emergency room when he was pronounced. Robert's father was an attending physician at the hospital and was in the emergency room that night.

A person of interest was identified as Markus Lockett, but there just wasn't enough evidence to charge him. He was later sentenced to twenty years in the Federal Penitentiary on drug charges. Robert Ellingwood's murder remains officially unsolved.

After the murder, there was a call for increased police presence on Dauphin Street. In December 1997, we moved our office from the Convention Center and opened the Central Events Precinct at 320 Dauphin Street. This was on the same corner where Robert Ellingwood had been murdered.

With the move to the new precinct building on Dauphin Street, we were more engaged with the business owners and patrons than we had been previously. There had always been a cordial, friendly relationship between us and the business owners (mostly) but having our precinct in the heart of the entertainment district changed everything for the better. Eventually, cameras were installed throughout the entertainment district, and we hired civilian camera operators to watch them 24 hours a day, 7 days a week. Every camera was recording onto a VHS tape, and those tapes had to be changed out daily and stored. In the late 1990s, that was top-of-the-line, cutting-edge technology. Now, digital recordings on servers that take up less space than a single day's use of VHS tapes are the norm.

Central Events Precinct early 2000s

On November 3, 2003, the Department opened the Police Museum inside the Central Events Precinct. The walls were murals of photographs from our history, and the showcases were filled with hundreds of donated items and documents dating back to the late 1800s. Over time, additional showcases were installed, and they housed items that were donated from police departments in the United Kingdom and Germany. The logbook had signatures of guests from around the world, and it was rare that the museum didn't have a guest looking around during the day.

The Mounted Unit was placed under the command of Central Events in 2011. This made sense because the primary operational area for the horses was downtown. By 2012, Central Events had grown from a three-person unit without a patrol car to a precinct commanded by a lieutenant and operated twenty-four hours a day, seven days a week with twenty-four officers and ten civilian employees.

In March of 2019, Central Events Unit was designated its own precinct and became Central Precinct and instead of being commanded by a lieutenant, a captain would be at the helm. A year later, in the spring of 2020, Mayor Sandy Stimpson decided to move the precinct off of Dauphin Street and into the ground floor of the RSA Tower. The entrance to the building would be on Water Street. Once the move took place, the camera operators were reassigned to other duties. There would be no twenty-four-hour monitoring of the camera systems any longer.

Additionally, the museum that had been showcasing our history to the public for nearly seventeen years was closed. Assistant Chief Roy Hodge and I packaged all of the museum items, cataloged them, and placed them in storage until a new facility can be found to operate as a museum.

Command of Central Events changed over the years. The commanders of Central Events are as follows:

- 1992-1994 the officers answered to Captain Hargrove in Precinct One.
- 1994-1995   Lieutenant Phillip Garrett (retired as Chief of Police)
- 1995-2001   Sergeant Craig Richards (died while in command)
- 2001-2003   Lieutenant Don Dixon (retired as Lieutenant)
- 2003-2006   Lieutenant David Mecurio (retired as Lieutenant)
- 2006-2010   Lieutenant Roy Hodge (retired as Interim Chief of Police)
- 2010-2012   Lieutenant Tommy Menton

(died while in command)
- 2012-2017   Lieutenant Billie L. Rowland (currently Captain, Commander, Precinct Four)
- 2017-2018   Lieutenant Ernest Treubig (currently Lieutenant, Precinct Two)
- 2018-2019   Lieutenant James Cunningham
- 2019-2021   Captain James Cunningham (currently Captain, Commander Special Operations)
- 2021-present   Captain Matthew Garrett (he is the son of the first Central Events lieutenant)

2002 Mardi Gras. George Cannon, Vincent Bertolino, Billie Rowland, Paul Alford, Jack Wilson, Robert Hudson

Mardi Gras 2002 Terry Hammoc, Bill Appling, Paul Alford,
Vincent Bertolino, Billie Rowland, Jamie Westbrook (center, front)

In 2013, the movie industry started making more movies in Mobile, mostly in the downtown area, and Central Events officers were used to shut down roadways and protect the film crew and stars as well as act as extras in the films. One of the first productions that came in that year was "Tokarev," though the name of the film changed to "Rage" after production. It starred Nicolas Cage, Rachel Nichols, and Danny Glover. The police department gave them two old patrol cars to use in the film (one of which was blown up), and several officers were used as extras with their patrol cars. Over the next few years, more than fifteen movies were made in Mobile, primarily in the downtown area. Well-known actors such as Bruce Willis, Gina Carano, and Robert Di Niro were protected by the Central Events officers. Nicolas Cage made several movies here during that time.

The Mobile Police Department was given high praise from the producers and directors of these films, and it was often stated how much more professional and friendly the officers were here compared to Los Angeles.

A scene from Rage in 2013

Set security for the chase and explosion scene

The following pages are photographs of the mural collages from the Police Museum when it was open at the Central Events Precinct.

As you can see from the units formed in the 1990s, Harold Johnson had a vision for law enforcement and how officers interacted and served the community. The cultural shift had begun. As with anything new, there would be growing pains. Feelings were hurt, morale was taking a hit, and the complaints about Johnson's leadership became more frequent. In less than two years, Johnson had been investigated by the FBI at least twice for complaints of abusing prisoners or improper orders issued to officers. Two grand jury investigations were held regarding complaints against him. He was cleared on all cases.

Johnson continued to run things his way, and he continued to rub just about everyone wrong. The Police Benevolent Association, the Black Police Benevolent Association, the Mobile County Law Enforcement Association, and numerous individual officers filed complaints and lawsuits against him. The Black Police Benevolent Association accused him of failing to promote minority officers in the percentages that they felt he should. The Mobile County Law Enforcement Association filed a suit against him for issuing General Order 55 which made it a major violation to criticize him, the mayor, or their policies. That General Order, known as the "Gag Order" stated "A member or employee shall not publicly criticize or ridicule the Mayor of the City, Chief of Police, the Executive Officers, the department or its policies, programs, actions, member or employees when such criticism or ridicule impairs the operation of the department or any command therein, or interfere with a supervisor's ability to maintain discipline." Johnson effectively made it a major violation of the rules of conduct subject to termination for criticizing him or the mayor. He did in fact fire an officer for voicing an opinion Johnson disagreed with. The officer who was fired was rehired a few years later. Though departments throughout the country had and have orders that prohibit false speech or the spreading of rumors, this order exceeded all of those and eliminated the officer's freedom of speech. The fallout surrounding it hit the national media and further impacted morale on the officers. The order was ultimately rescinded.

In 1991, Mobile had a nineteen percent increase in felony crimes. The public was tired of the high crime, the officers were tired of the low pay and lower morale, and everyone blamed Harold Johnson. He stood strong and took the hits. He held to his vision and kept moving forward. He continued to have missteps, like hiring Frank DeCrease to be his administrative assistant. This was the same position DeCrease had when he worked for Johnson in Michigan.

Despite the missteps, the Department did see some improvement, not only in manpower allocated and new units being formed, but in obtaining law enforcement accreditation from the Commission on Accreditation for Law Enforcement Agencies, "CALEA," in the late summer of 1994. To obtain the accreditation, a department must meet more than seven hundred nationally recognized standards. The department, its personnel, records, policies, and procedures are inspected by CALEA investigators to ensure the department meets the high standards. At the time Mobile PD obtained the accreditation, the only other department in the State of Alabama to also be accredited was Birmingham. To this day, the MPD has maintained the standards and kept the accreditation rating.

The vision for change that Ruben Greenburg, Harold Johnson, and the men and women of the Mobile Police Department who were tired of the way things had been operating was realized. They succeeded in their goals of changing the culture of this agency. It can be said that with all of Johnson's faults, his leadership changed the course of the Department history for the better. The only thing that didn't readily improve under his administration was the Department's morale.

Harold Johnson retired from the Department due to medical issues on June 27, 1996. He remained in Mobile. In 1998 the City Council voted to rename Police Headquarters after him, and it is now known as the Harold L. Johnson Police Headquarters Building.

On Wednesday, May 22, 2008, Harold Johnson passed away.

Notable Arrests

Patricia Krenwinkel

On August 9th, 1969, in Los Angeles, California, Sharon Tate (actress), Jay Sebring (hair stylist), Abigail Folger (heiress to the Folger coffee company), Wojiciech "Voytek" Frykowski (boyfriend of Abigail), and Stephen Parent (an eighteen-year-old male in the wrong place at the wrong time), were killed at 10050 Cielo Drive. The murders shocked the nation because of the victims as well as the gruesomeness of the killings. Sharon was eight months pregnant at the time and was married to movie director Roman Polanski.

On August 10, 1969, grocery store owner Leno LaBianca and his wife Rosemary were murdered in the same manner at their home at 3301 Waverly Drive, also in Los Angeles.

These murders would become known as the Manson Murders, but at the time, the investigation was just beginning. After months of investigating leads, some suspects were developed. One of them was a young, twenty-one-year-old female named Patricia Krenwinkel. Her father was an insurance agent who lived in Inglewood, California. He told officers that Patricia was in Mobile, Alabama, staying with her mother. Patricia had lived in Mobile for a time after her parents divorced. She had attended Theodore High School her junior year, and she attended Springhill College for a semester before moving back to California.

In late November 1969, the LAPD reached out to Chief James Robinson and asked for assistance in locating Patricia Krenwinkel. Captain Don Riddle, who supervised investigations, assigned detectives to the case. (Don Riddle would become chief in 1974).

On December 1, 1969, Sergeant McKellar and an unknown partner were staking out an address on Bucknell Drive, where it was believed Krenwinkel was staying. The property belonged to her aunt. The officers spotted a small sports car approach them driven by a young male, and the female passenger pulled her hat down to cover her face. The vehicle was stopped, and the female identified herself as Mary Montgomery. When the officers took her to her aunt's house, she confessed that her name was Patricia Krenwinkel.

According to Vincent Bugliosi in his book "Helter Skelter," which was written after he prosecuted the Manson Family for the murders, a key piece of evidence was provided by the Mobile Police Department. He states that their case became stronger because Mobile Police Sergeant Sam McLarty fingerprinted Krenwinkel and sent them the prints. Upon receiving the prints from Mobile, they were able to match the print of the little finger on Krenwinkel's left hand to a print that was lifted on a door inside Sharon Tate's bedroom.

December 9, 1969

James J. Robinson, Chief of Police
Mobile Police Department
Mobile, Alabama 36600

Dear Sir:

Enclosed is a certified copy of our Superior Court bench warrant
(indictment) #A253156 which charges PATRICIA KRENWINKEL aka Mary
Ann Scott and numerous other aliases with 7 counts of murder and
1 count of criminal conspiracy, the maximum sentence for which
punishable by death or life imprisonment.

This subject is presently in your custody, and being held for the
Los Angeles Police Department on their warrant. We therefore request
that our warrant be placed as additional detainer against her.

We would appreciate your acknowledging the receipt of our warrant,
and in the event that the Los Angeles Police Department is not
successful in their extradition of subject, please advise if she
will waive extradition. If she will not, we will when so notified,
commence formal extradition.

If subject is no longer in your custody please forward for this
department to the holding agency.

Please direct inquiries or replies regarding this letter to the
Sheriff's Department, Fugitive/Warrant Detail, Detective Division,
Special Units Bureau, Hall of Justice, Los Angeles, California 90012.

Thank you for your consideration and assistance in this matter, and
please be assured of the cooperation of this department at all times.

Sincerely,

PETER J. PITCHESS, SHERIFF

F. G. Fimbres

F. G. Fimbres, Chief
Detective Division

ADDRESS ALL COMMUNICATIONS TO PETER J. PITCHESS, SHERIFF

KRENWINKEL, Patricia

December 11, 1969

Chief of Police

Honorable Peter J. Pitchess,
Sheriff of Los Angeles County,
Los Angeles, California 90012.

Re: 069-28737-2046-286

Attention: F. G. Fimbres, Chief of Detectives

Dear Sir:

Please be advised that we received your warrant
for Patricia Krenwinkel this date and turned same over
to our District Attorney, Mr. Carl M. Booth, who is in
constant contact with the District Attorney's Office
in Los Angeles.

Also assuring you that it has been a pleasure to
have assisted you in this matter, I remain,

Very truly yours,

James J. Robinson,
Chief of Police

JJR:ep

State of California
GOVERNOR'S OFFICE
SACRAMENTO 95814

RONALD REAGAN
GOVERNOR

December 12, 1969

The Honorable Albert P. Brewer
Governor of Alabama
State Capitol
Montgomery, Alabama

Dear Governor Brewer:

At the request of Acting Governor Reinecke, I am enclos-
ing an extradition requisition for the return of
PATRICIA KRENWINKEL to the State of California.

If this requisition is honored by you, will you please
forward the necessay papers and the agent's appointment
to the Chief of Police, Mobile, Alabama.

Kindly notify the Honorable Evelle J. Younger, District
Attorney of Los Angeles County, 600 Hall of Justice,
Los Angeles, California (Attention: Miss Elvyn Holt,
Chief, Extradition Section), by collect wire of your
action in this matter.

Sincerely,

Herbert E. Ellingwood
Legal Affairs Secretary

HEE:jr

Enclosures

cc: Hon. Evelle J. Younger

Chief of Police, Mobile, Alabama

Krenwinkel and the other members of the Manson Family were convicted and sentenced to death. California repealed the death penalty shortly after this, and all of the convictions were commuted to life. As of this writing, Krenwinkel is still incarcerated.

I have searched for the fingerprint card and have not been able to locate it. It is not known if the only card was sent to Los Angeles or if it was taken/lost from the archives. The case in California was so sensational and has been etched in time that our link to it could not be ignored. When the police museum was designed and placed in the Central Events police precinct at 320 Dauphin Street, a photograph of the arrest and case was displayed in the form of a mural on a set of folding doors. The museum has now closed, but the doors are safely stored for future display. The following is a photograph of the mural.

Patricia Krenwinkel

Vernon Johnson

St. Valentine's Day, February 14, 1972, was also Lundi Gras in Mobile. That day would become known in Mobile as our own St. Valentine's Day Massacre. The King Felix and Floral parades had ended and there would be a break before the evening parades started. The employees of the Mutual Finance Company loan office at 54 South Conception Street returned to work from watching the parades. It was about 3 pm. One of the employees, Gaybrielle Hattenstein, was on the telephone with a customer when she suddenly stated that she was being robbed and asked the customer to call the police. The customer called the police, and they were enroute within minutes. One of the officers was only two blocks from the scene when the call was dispatched.

As the officers entered the business, they heard cries for help coming from the back of the store. Once they entered the combination restroom/storage room, they found five people suffering from gunshots. Two men and three women had been forced into the room by a robber and then shot. One male and one female had been shot in the head and were deceased. One female had been shot in the jaw; a male customer had been shot in the shoulder; and Ms. Hattenstein had been shot in the neck and was paralyzed.

A description was broadcast of a Black male, early 20s, five-feet-two to five- feet-five inches tall, one hundred twenty pounds, dressed in a businessman's black suit, wearing a plaid shirt, and green velvet hat. He was carrying a zippered bag in which he had placed the $300 he had stolen.

As time passed, no new leads developed, and the case was going cold. It was a nearly forgotten case, but on October 21, 1973, the killer struck again. That Sunday evening, just after dark, around 6:50 pm, a short Black male entered Naman's Super Market at 563 South Broad Street. The male pointed a gun at Elias Naman and ordered him to call the stockboy, Larry Kling, from the back of the store. He then handed Naman a zippered bag and demanded money from the safe and the register.

After receiving the money, he ordered Mr. Naman and Kling into Naman's station wagon. Naman was forced to drive, Kling was in the passenger seat, and the robber was in the back seat. They drove from the scene. As they did so, the female employee at the store called the police.

Officer Lanier was driving a paddy wagon that night and spotted the car as he was crossing a roadway. He backed up and began pursuing the vehicle. Before Officer Lanier could catch up to them, the robber ordered Naman to stop the car. As the vehicle was slowing to a stop, on Marine Street near Church Street, the robber shot both Naman and Kling in the back of the head. Kling was killed instantly, Mr. Naman lingered for almost two days before passing.

The suspect fled the vehicle on foot, shedding clothing and throwing the handgun away as he ran. He ran into the parking lot at 951 Government Street and attempted to hide in a small garden that had been built around a tree. Officer Kenneth Watts spotted the suspect lying on his stomach and was able to take him into custody. Under his body was the zippered bag. Inside the bag, $1,154 in cash was found inside a Naman's bank bag that had been prepared for the night deposit. The .38 revolver was found where it had been dropped. The investigation fell to Captain Kater Williams, and once he arrived on the scene, he later stated that he made a mental note to check this suspect out on the Mutual Finance case.

The suspect was identified as Vernon Johnson, a twenty-five-year-old psychology student at Bishop State College. During the interrogation and initial investigation, Identification Lieutenant McLarty (noted in the Krenwinkel arrest as Sergeant McLarty) walked into Captain Williams' office with a piece of evidence that had been recovered. The zippered bag that was recovered that night had a striking resemblance to the zippered bag described in the Mutual Finance case.

Vernon Johnson was charged with four murders, three attempted murders, and three robberies. He was ultimately convicted on all counts, and he was sentenced to life in prison. He currently resides at the Fountain Correctional Facility and has had several parole hearings in which he has been denied release at each of them. His next parole hearing is scheduled for April 1, 2026.

Rickey Prewitt and Paul Leverett

This case highlights the cooperation between the Mobile Police Department, the District Attorney's Office, and the FBI. In the early 1980s, our investigators worked with these outside agencies to solve some high-profile crimes, such as the Michael Donald murder on Herndon Avenue, and the following case, and bring criminals to justice.

On May 30, 1980, Paul Leverett, the co-owner of Colonel Dixie restaurants, took his son and daughter to lunch at Constantine's Restaurant and then to purchase a car for his son. They returned to their home on Montcliff Drive around 4 pm.

Inside the bedroom, Paul found his wife, Elizabeth, murdered. She had been shot twice and stabbed. Paul first called family and then the police.

Mobile Police officers arrived on the scene and conducted the investigation. The coroner found that Elizabeth had been shot in the face and in the neck. The bullet that struck her neck first travelled through her left hand indicating she was defending herself. The killer also slashed her face with a knife and cut her throat four times. It was a violent death and indicated it was a known person filled with rage. According to Major Sam McLarty, Elizabeth was not having an affair, and the belief was the husband was somehow involved, but he had an airtight alibi.

Clues were slow to come in, and the case seemed to dry up until some tips started coming in from a bar located on South Broad Street. The tipsters stated that a wealthy man had been asking around for someone to burglarize his home, and there were rumors that this man wanted the burglar to kill his wife. Officers were able to confirm that Paul Leverett was a frequent customer of the bar. They believed he was involved but there were still too many missing pieces.

Several months went by with little development and then a small break in the case happened. Some silver, which had been reported stolen from a home in Point Clear, had been reportedly sold in New Orleans. A family member went to New Orleans and spotted some of the stolen items in a store window on Magazine Street. She told the owner of the store that it had been stolen and asked him to hold it until the police could investigate.

The department did not immediately respond to the request to drive to New Orleans to investigate as it appeared to be unrelated. The District Attorney at the time, Chris Galanos, had just hired Bob Eddy as an investigator, and he sent Eddy to New Orleans to look into the silver theft. Bob Eddy spoke to the shop owner and was told that the silver was bought from a man named Hilton Robinson and that Robinson operated a flea market on Government Boulevard in Mobile. It was discovered that the FBI was looking into Robinson for other crimes, so Eddy and FBI Agent Rich Reeves began working together. The case was still not linked to the murder.

Robinson was convicted of transporting stolen property across state lines and sentenced to twelve years in the Federal Penitentiary. Shortly after this, U.S. Attorney Jeff Sessions, called the Mobile Police and D.A. Galanos and told them that Robinson claimed to have information on the Leverett murder.

After several interviews, Robinson stated that Rickey Prewitt was involved in the murder of Elizabeth Leverett, stating that Prewitt confessed as much to him and that he gave him a diamond ring to fence. A diamond ring had been stolen from the hand of Mrs. Leverett at the time of the murder, but that information had not been released.

In December 1981, Galanos had a Grand Jury look into the case. The Grand Jury interviewed witnesses, including Paul Leverett's new wife Phyllis. Paul and Phyllis had married six months after the murder, and it was rumored they had been having an affair prior to the murder. Phyllis was married to another man at the time of the murder and was living in Grand Bay, Alabama. D.A. Galanos believed that Phyllis lied during the Grand Jury testimony, and he indicted her for perjury. At her trial for perjury, the judge hearing the case issued a direct verdict of acquittal which infuriated law enforcement. It was their belief that the judge did so due to Paul Leverett's relationship with several of the judges. Leverett had taken many of them on hunting trips over the years.

The case was re-presented to a Grand Jury and that jury returned indictments against Rickey Prewitt and Paul Leverett for capital murder. Prewitt was tried in Mobile beginning in January 1983. Prewitt was convicted of capital murder and sentenced to life without parole. Soon after his conviction, Prewitt started talking to investigators, revealing information into the killing.

Prewitt stated that he was paid $10,000 to kill Elizabeth Leverett by Paul Leverett. He stated that William McEvoy was the intermediary, and that McEvoy had provided him with keys to the house. On the day of the murder, he used the keys to enter the home and hide in the closet until Elizabeth returned.

Paul Leverett's trial was moved to Montgomery, Alabama. Before the trial, additional information was obtained that led to the indictment of William McEvoy as an accomplice to the murder. McEvoy pleaded guilty to conspiracy to murder and was sentenced to ten years in prison. At Paul Leverett's trial, McEvoy testified that he had worked with Leverett to set up the murder with Prewitt. In May 1983, Leverett was convicted of murder and sentenced to life in prison.

On October 23, 1994, Leverett was being housed at the state cattle ranch in Hale County. He was a trustee and assigned duties as a hunting dog trainer. On that day, an inmate broke into the warden's house where he killed the warden, his wife, and set the house of fire. Leverett and another inmate were near the house when this occurred, and as the suspect fled, he shot both of them with a shotgun, killing them instantly.

Samuel Ivery

In the early afternoon of August 15, 1992, Samuel Ivery entered the Shell Gas Station located on the northeast corner of Government Street and Broad Street. He waited inside the store for about thirty minutes for the store to clear of customers. Once the store was empty, he locked the doors from the inside. He robbed the clerk, twenty-seven-year-old Deborah Lewis, of $302 and then forced her to the floor. He bound her wrists with duct tape, covered her mouth and eyes with duct tape, and then decapitated her with a hatchet.

He was seen running from the store with what a witness thought was blood on his shirt. He was carrying a travel bag. Another witness later saw him in a grocery store north of downtown, washing his clothes in the bathroom sink. That witness observed the travel bag and saw a hatchet and knife inside it. Ivery told him he kept the items for protection.

The following day, Sergeant Joe Connick spotted the suspect walking down Government Street. As he stopped to question the suspect, Ivery led him on a foot chase throughout the downtown area. He was apprehended by Officer Karl Reed.

Over the next few days, officers searched the area for the travel bag and weapons. I was in the police academy, Class 16, at the time, and we were about to graduate. The chief came to the academy and told us we would be deployed to the area where Ivery was last thought to be, to conduct grid searches and searches of abandoned buildings. We did not find anything in our search.

On August 12, 1992, twelve days after the incident, the travel bag was found in an abandoned house at 1161 Dr. Martin Luther King Avenue. It contained the knife, hatchet, and other items used in the murder. Samuel Ivery's fingerprints were found on the weapons.

On October 15, 1992, the "St. Louis Dispatch" printed an article about Samuel Ivery. He had been linked to two murders in the St. Louis, Missouri, area. In both murders, the female victims had been decapitated. One of these victims was only seventeen years old. She was murdered on July 25, 1992. The other victim was thirty-one, and she was murdered on July 15, 1992. He was later indicted for these murders but never tried.

Samuel Ivery was convicted of murder and sentenced to die in the electric chair. Samuel Ivery killed himself in prison in 1996.

Stories from the Field

Anyone who has worked in law enforcement knows that the job is filled with monotony. It is not wide-open, chasing bad guys, making big arrests every day. Most days are spent responding to the same type of calls: domestics, accidents, shoplifting, or nuisance complaints. There is always danger and the great probability that something will break loose during the shift. Emotionally, an officer can be spent at the end of a shift, feeling drained from being on alert all day and solving the problems of others. If you are in this job long enough, you will see and experience things that will have a profound effect on you.

There are times when something happens that is burned into your memory. Maybe not because it was extreme violence or because of the danger surrounding the call, it may just be something that was unusual or funny at the time. Police officers often have an unusual sense of humor. It is a coping mechanism for years spent seeing the worst in people, seeing what violence and trauma does to the human body, and dealing with the dangerous elements of society. Our humor is a coping mechanism for helping us get through these events. It allows us to push on, handling the call with professionalism without becoming attached to the situation.

The following are stories, collected from veteran officers—retired and former. The stories may be something that stood out to them as odd, or it may be something that they found funny. These stories cover decades of policing, so some of the ways calls are described here may not be what is acceptable today. They are included here to pass on the oral history of the Mobile Police Department. We cannot forget that it is the people who make up the history of the department. It is their lives, in years of service or in physical body, that make the department what it is and what it will become. These are their stories.

Domestic on Flicker

One of my first calls out of the police academy was a domestic on Flicker Street. It was the afternoon shift, and we hadn't been on patrol for long. Dispatch stated that there was a domestic involving one cut. As we were pulling up to the address, we could see a Black male with his arms around a Black female, and it appeared they were hugging. It did not look like there was a struggle, but as we approached on foot, it became clear that the female was covered in blood. My FTO (field training officer) and me grabbed the male and put handcuffs on him. The female started losing her mind that we were arresting him, when we noticed he was also bleeding from multiple stab wounds.

As we waited on the paramedics to arrive, we were able to determine what had occurred. Our male suspect started an argument with his wife because he could not find the car keys. She didn't have them, and her answers weren't good enough for him, so he yanked the window air conditioner out of the window and threw it at her. He then grabbed a hammer and tried to attack her. Our female victim had had enough of this, and she grabbed a knife from the kitchen and proceeded to stab him multiple times. He took the knife from her and stabbed her.

When we had arrived and saw them embracing, they were apologizing to each other and expressing their love for one another. Neither one would accept medical treatment, and they both refused to cooperate with the report. In those days, one of the parties would have to sign the warrant, unlike today where we can make arrests, and sign warrants on domestic violence cases if we see indications of violence. When it was all said and done, I looked in their car and saw the keys in the ignition.

State Street Hotel

One night shift, I was riding downtown when me and another officer decided to check inside an abandoned hotel at State Street and Joachim Street. This building was frequently used by the homeless, drug addicts, and prostitutes. As we entered and began searching, we heard noises coming from the second floor. When we got to the room that was occupied, we shined our lights in and saw two males, buck naked having sex. After we had them dress, we walked them down to our patrol cars, placing one in each vehicle. I ran the subject in my car and my backing officer ran the other in his on PD Main.

After a few minutes, the dispatcher gave my backing officer his subject check. I noticed that his subject had the same last name as mine. Well, they did indeed have the same last name, because they were brothers. To make things worse, one of them was the fry cook at Popeye's at the Loop. They were both taken in for wandering abroad (vagrancy.) I didn't eat at that Popeye's for years after that.

Kellogg Street Stabbing

One midnight shift I was riding 12's beat when I was dispatched to a shots fired call in 18's beat on Kellogg Street. There was no complainant to see, and there was frequent gunfire in the area, so I responded without a backing unit. When I turned onto Kellogg Street, I didn't see or hear anything, but a few houses down, as I was shining my spotlight, I saw what appeared to be blood on a door and doorstep. It looked like someone had taken a bucket of red paint and dumped it out. As my spotlight illuminated the grass on the side of the house, I saw a body. I called for additional units and medical to start to the scene.

I approached the male who was only wearing pants and one shoe. It was dimly lit in the area, but with my Maglite, I was able to see that he had been stabbed multiple times. His intestines were hanging out and were spread out nearly ten feet behind where he laid. It looked like he had been stabbed, fell to the ground, got up and ran, was caught, stabbed again, falling, and running until he reached this final location. He was still alive.

I followed the ambulance to USA Medical Center and was in the trauma room as the doctors worked on him. He was answering questions and cooperating with me and the doctors. He gave me his name, date of birth, and social security number. Homicide was notified because it didn't look like he would survive. Twenty-eight stab wounds were counted, intestines punctured and shredded. I walked outside to start my report and to run him on PD Main.

Knowing he was most likely going to die, his last words before going into surgery were lies. He lied about who he was, he gave a false name, date of birth and social security number. He lived. It turned out, he was selling bunk to some of the neighborhood thugs, and they came back for revenge. They were never caught. I still do not know why the call came in about shots fired. We found no evidence that a gun was used or fired.

Several years later, I was a lieutenant working the First Precinct and I backed one of my officers on a suspicious call involving a Black male possibly selling drugs in the area of Ann Steet and Duval Street. It was him, still living in the projects, still selling drugs.

Foot, the Homeless Man

While working downtown, we had occasion to get to know most—if not all—of the homeless in the area. Most were a real pain in the ass. Not only for the citizens, but for the police as well. One homeless man was the exception. He was a massive man, full beard, heavy set, and filthy dirty. He smelled terrible and refused to bathe. We laughed because he smelled like "foot in the ass", so we called him Foot. He was cordial and even joked with us about calling him Foot.

Foot never begged for money, never got in the way, and if asked, he would politely leave where he was not wanted. One day, Foot was pushing his shopping cart filled with all his worldly belongings down Claiborne Street. He saw two males harassing a couple of females as they walked from the parking lot towards Dauphin Street. When one of the guys grabbed one of the females, Foot had seen enough. He grabbed the male and slung him to the ground and then went after the other guy that was standing there in shock. The girls ran to the corner and then into the Central Events Precinct. Foot had scared them as much as the two guys had. When we arrived on scene, Foot was gone, and the two male suspects were gone. The girls were still a bit shaken. After hearing their story and description of the man who saved them, we were able to calm them down. We told them about Foot and that he was harmless. They went on their way to the bars.

We reviewed the camera footage, and it captured some of the event. It was most certainly Foot, and he did jump in to save these girls from any harm. He was last seen slowly pushing his cart north on Claiborne Street. We felt it was important to recognize him for his deed. We typed up an official Commander's Citation on award paper, documenting his good deed. A few days later, we saw him pushing his cart down the street, and we were able to present him with his certificate. He smiled like he had just won a great award. It wasn't long after, he just disappeared.

Halls Mill Road Kidnapping

On July 4, 1995, I was riding 12's beat on day shift. My dad was riding along that day. I was dispatched to a house on Halls Mill Road in reference to the caller's girlfriend pointing a gun at him. Neil Baker was my backing unit. We arrived and approached the front door. The male caller stepped outside but kept his foot inside the door. He stated that his girlfriend had come over to the house that morning and pointed a gun at him and then she left. His story and demeanor did not really add up, so I continued to question him. After a few minutes, he stepped outside fully, letting the front door close.

As we continued to ask him questions, he became more evasive. All the while, he was slowly walking towards the carport. As we were on the carport, I heard something inside the house at the door. I looked and saw a female figure trying to get out the door. She was wrapped in coaxial cable and her hands were bound with duct tape. She had duct tape covering her mouth. I immediately grabbed the suspect's arm and Neil grabbed the other. The fight was on. We couldn't get him under control. I grabbed my baton and began striking him in the back and shoulder, trying to get him to comply. He calmly asked why I was hitting him.

As we struggled to get him under control, we were making our way into the front yard. We each had an arm but couldn't get him cuffed. My dad jumped out of the car and ran towards us to assist. After a few strikes to the face, our suspect gave up. When he was secured in the car, I went to the house and untied the female.

She told us that she had been dating our suspect for a while and that the night before, he came to her apartment and forced her into his car. He drove her to his house and tied her up. He told her that he was going to call the police and tell them that she threatened him with a gun. He told her after the police departed, he was going to kill her and claim she had returned. He forced her to hold a pistol so her fingerprints would be on it.

The detectives arrived and while we were inside the house, we found over a kilo of cocaine and nearly $20,000 in cash. He was charged with kidnapping, assault, and attempted murder, along with the resisting and drug charges. Ultimately, he was prosecuted for crimes in the Federal system related to drugs and guns where he was sentenced to life without parole.

Several years later, we arrested the female victim for stealing cars and transporting them to Louisiana.

Mustang Sally's

In the mid-1990s, there was a bar in the parking area of Bel Air Mall called Mustang Sally's. It was a popular hangout for a young crowd. One night, we received a call about a disorderly in the parking lot. It had been called in by the bouncer.

When we pulled into the parking lot, we could see a crowd gathered by a parked car. As we approached on foot, we heard hear a male screaming and begging as if he were in great pain. We made our way through the crowd and finally saw why the male was crying in agony. He was wearing nylon jogging pants and a t-shirt, standing with his face toward the open door of a car. Inside the car was a quite attractive young female. She had a determined, angry look about her. It was then we saw the rest. She had his balls in her hands and was hanging on to them with all of her might. It took some convincing but once we handcuffed the male, she let go of his testicles.

It seemed that this young man had found our female "victim" attractive—attractive enough for him to force his way into her open door in an attempt to get on top of her. She apparently didn't find him worthy of her affections, and she grabbed his balls. She squeezed them as hard as she could and kept squeezing until we arrested him. I don't think he will try that again.

Dauphin Street Accident

On Sunday, July 11, 1993, I was working downtown for the Southern Legislative Leadership Conference. State representatives and senators from all over the Southeast were in town for the conference, and I was assigned to patrol Dauphin Street to keep a visible presence and to keep the vagrants away from the restaurants and parks.

I was riding a Honda Elite scooter that day. The scooters were a step above a moped, but definitely not a motorcycle. The wheels were small, and it didn't sit very high, but it did get great gas mileage and up to 50 miles an hour, if you were brave enough. As I was driving down Dauphin Street, doing the speed limit of 25 mph, I approached the intersection of Joachim Street. As I entered the intersection, I saw, coming from the left, a car that should have stopped for the light. There was no way to stop or avoid the collision, and I impacted the right front quarter panel of the offending car. As I flew over the hood of the car, everything was in slow motion. I remember vividly, seeing the old man's face. The look of shock and fear on it indicated he was as alarmed as I was. I distinctly remember thinking "Shit, this is going to hurt".

The next thing I knew, I was waking up in the emergency room. I was strapped to a back board, my neck in a c-collar, and tape from my forehead to the board. It felt as though my right side was on fire. It was an excruciating pain, and I thought the road rash must be terrible. So many thoughts run through your head in these instances, and it doesn't take long to come up with every possible bad possibility.

As I was lying there for what seemed to be forever (I am sure it was only for a few moments), the doctor came in and stood over me. While he was talking, I saw that he had tears in his eyes and was choking on his words. A wave of terror flooded over me in that instant. I thought it must be horrendous if the doctor is crying.

As all the terrible possibilities were swirling in my head, I heard him choke up and say, "What the hell is that crap?" Before too much confusion could register in my mind about his comment, I heard a voice from an unseen officer behind me. He said "That is his pepper spray. The canister blew up when he hit the ground."

I was never so relieved in all my life! The officer stepped up, looking down with a smile and a laugh, Lieutenant Barton started to make fun of me. He did tell me that the old man was alright and that he was in town for the conference. He was a senator from Mississippi. I was having a rough day, but Barton was having one as well. He was at the hospital dealing with my injury and accident, but he hadn't even finished the mess he had to deal with from earlier in the shift. One of his officers had pulled up to the Circle K store on Michigan and Melrose that morning and he saw a young Black male run from the store, carrying the cash register. The officer gave chase, and the suspect dropped the cash register but continued running. The officer was gaining on him when he observed what he thought was the suspect trying to point a gun at him. The officer fired, striking the suspect in the butt.

After a few laughs at my painful circumstances, I was taken back for tests. After a while, I was discharged and sent home. As I got into the shower, hoping to clean the road debris and pepper spray from my body, the hot water reactivated the pepper spray, and the steam made it even worse than before. Hours of discomfort lay ahead, but I finally got past the pain of that chemical agent.

The next morning, I woke up but couldn't move. Everything hurt, and I had no ability so sit up or stand. After a few minutes, I rolled out of the bed and crawled into the living room to the telephone. I called my supervisor, Captain Hargrove, who stated that he had word I was still in the hospital. I assured him that I wasn't and was in my apartment. He sent two officers to pick me up and take me back to the hospital. When we arrived, the nurse at the front desk said I was listed as being in a room upstairs. Somehow, they discharged me while simultaneously checking me into the hospital.

After a few days, I went back to work and when I got to the office, I picked up my gun belt and other equipment that had been taken off of me the day of the accident. I went straight to work, and it wasn't long into the shift that I had used the radio. It was July in the deep south, working outside, so obviously I was sweating. As I wiped the sweat from my face and eyes, an instant burning sensation hit like a freight train. The pepper spray had coated my radio but dried, so I was unaware. The sweat reactivated it on my hands and then face. To this day I refuse to carry that godawful chemical.

Teen vs Train

The day of Walter Jackson's retirement party at the First Precinct, I and other officers enjoyed reminiscing with Walter and wishing him the best in his retirement. As the party was wrapping up, there was only about an hour until the end of the shift, so me and another officer decided to head to the Hill. The Hill was just that, a hill, right in the curve of Broad Street and Commander's Drive. In the 1990s, it was a vacant lot, elevated, and surrounded by trees. It was a great place to get out of the public view for a while, and it was a meeting place for after shift "choir practices" as well. Today, it is an Airbus facility and parking lot.

As we made our way down Broad Street, we were stopped at the train tracks near Tennessee Street. I was first in line, and Pat was stopped behind me. As the train was passing, I observed several teenagers running along the moving train from the right. They crossed in front of me and continued on towards Washington Avenue. The train continued for a few minutes and as soon as it passed, I began driving over the tracks. Something caught my eye to the left, I looked but couldn't quite make out what it was. I stopped my patrol car and looked again. It still didn't register what I was seeing along those tracks, so I turned my patrol car and drove towards the object on the ground a few hundred feet away.

As I put the car in park and exited, it became clear to me that what I thought I saw was indeed what I was seeing now. One of the teenagers who had just run past me was lying on his back with his butt nearly touching the tracks. What was missing were his legs. As he lay there, two nubs were left, his legs removed just below the groin. There wasn't any blood, he wasn't screaming or saying anything at all. Pat, being a former ambulance medic, went to him and began keeping his head stable and focused on him, not looking down at his severed limbs.

I immediately called dispatch via the radio, requesting medical assistance, as well at traffic investigators and additional backing officers. While they were en route, I found the severed limbs, marking their location in the gravel and bringing them closer to the teenager in hopes that something could be done to save them. I marked the location of the first limb and dropped it off. As I was walking the one hundred twenty feet to the second limb, I heard the sergeant on the radio. She was cancelling all responding units and medical. It took me a millisecond to become enraged that she would cancel them, so I keyed up the radio and forcefully told the dispatcher to keep everyone en route. The sergeant again keyed the radio and tried to cancel the responding units, stating that she was at Broad Street and Texas Street and there were no train tracks at that location. I yelled into the radio that we were at Broad Street and TENNESSEE STREET and that we needed medical quickly.

I marked the location of the second severed leg and was walking back to where Pat, the teenager, and the other limb were waiting when Captain Hargrove pulled up. As I approached, leg still in hand, Captain Hargrove looked me square in the face and said "Now, now, you need to get your hat on." No questions about how the kid was, what we had found, nothing about the scene, just worrying about the damn hat.

Lt. Frank Woodard and officers from the Identification Unit, traffic officers, medical, and other backing officers began pouring in. The sergeant who cancelled the responding backing officers arrived on scene and immediately relieved me and Pat from the call. She ordered us to go 10-8 to answer calls. I was just a few years into my career at MPD at that time and if it weren't for some veteran officers and supervisors like Mike Barton, I would have most likely quit over that. I realized at that time, not everyone at MPD was the quality that I expected for our agency, and I was determined to make a difference.

Sixteen or seventeen years later, I stopped a car driving down Broad Street for what I though was a DUI. As I approached the car and shined my light into the driver's compartment, I saw the driver had no legs. He was using wooden broom handles to manipulate the gas and brake pedals. After a short conversation, it was revealed that this was the teenager from years ago. He still lived in the same house with his parents and seemed to have adjusted to life without his legs.

Pursuit

In May 2008 I was a sergeant in Precinct Four on night shift. It had been a quiet night for a weekend. At about 2200 hours, one of my officers notified dispatch that he was attempting to stop a GMC Envoy that was observed speeding out of a parking lot at a nightclub. The driver refused to stop. Officer Booth did a great job calling the pursuit, speeds were not excessive, and the roadway traffic was light.

The pursuit travelled west on Airport Boulevard and then back to the east. I was ahead of the pursuit, so I parked my patrol car near the intersection of Airport Boulevard and Azalea Road, and grabbed the Stop Sticks from the trunk. I could see the officers' lights as they topped the hill west of my location, and I advised that I was going to deploy the Stop Sticks. The officers slowed and allowed the suspect to get a little distance between them. As he approached my position, I deployed the sticks. The suspect swerved towards me, nearly striking my patrol car and in doing so, missed the deflation device. I quickly pulled them back out of the roadway to prevent an officer from striking them as they quickly passed by. They reengaged with the suspect vehicle, and I jumped back into my car and began catching up to the pursuing vehicles.

As I passed the intersection of Office Park Drive, Officer Booth notified dispatch that the suspect was turning right on Downtowner Boulevard. The suspect had increased his speed to over 90 miles per hour, and by the time I made the turn onto Downtowner Boulevard, Officer Booth stated that they were approaching Michael Boulevard.

Just after I passed Downtowner Loop South, Officer Booth came over the air saying the suspect had wrecked out. The next words on the radio were "Fire." Other officers started asking for the fire department and medical. As I was rolling up, I saw Officer Booth with a fire extinguisher putting out a fire in the engine compartment of the GMC. The vehicle was on its passenger side, wrapped around an oak tree. The vehicle had slid sideways, passenger side into the oak tree with such violence that it wrapped around the tree, flipping up onto its side, crushing the roof into the passenger compartment.

You could not see the driver from outside the vehicle due to the way the vehicle was crushed around him. Corporal Miller crawled through the broken back glass of the SUV and checked on the driver. He stated that he appeared to be deceased.

Mobile Fire Medics and an Engine Company arrived on the scene in short order, and the medics made entry into the vehicle through the same broken window that Corporal Miller had just exited. They also confirmed that the suspect was deceased.

I began making the notifications to the Captain and to Deputy Chief Kennedy. Traffic Homicide and the Identification Unit were requested as well as an impound wrecker. As this was taking place, the scene was being secured and attempts to identify the driver were being made. We were still unable to get to the driver. To do so, we would have to pull the vehicle off of the tree, back onto its wheels, and then cut the crushed metal roof away from the passenger compartment. It was going to be a long process.

As all of this was taking place, I had Officer Booth sit in his car and begin writing his narrative of the events while they were still fresh in his mind and to keep him away from the death scene. The dispatcher called over the radio asking for units to clear to take a report of a stolen vehicle. The location of the theft was the same parking lot where this pursuit began. Officers arrived on that scene and discovered that the vehicle that was stolen was actually the vehicle that we were out with. That answered the question of why the driver was refusing to stop.

Identification officers and Traffic officers arrived on the scene and began photographing and measuring the scene. Once all of the preliminary investigations were completed, we were ready to pull the vehicle off of the tree. The wrecker driver hooked up to the GMC and tried to pull it off of the tree, but the way it was wrapped around it, it would not budge. After readjusting the cables and chains, the wrecker was able to pry the vehicle off of the tree and back onto its wheels.

The fire medics attempted to get into the passenger compartment again but were still prevented due to the damage. The fire department began cutting the wreckage apart to gain access to the driver's compartment. They cut the pillars and made some other cuts in the sheet metal giving them enough leeway to pull the roof off of the vehicle. We were all standing close to the vehicle as the firemen began pulling the metal off of the crushed compartment and freeing the driver. As they made a final pull of the roof, a loud gasp could be heard and then "Get me the fuck out of here!" Everyone standing there looked at each other wondering who made the gasp and yelled to be released. We all stared at the now suddenly alive driver. For over two hours, he had no signs of life, but now that the pressure of the roof was relieved, he was alive and vocal.

Even though the driver's compartment was exposed, and the driver could be given initial medical attention, he could not be removed. The dash and steering wheel were crushed around his hips and legs. It was going to take some time to cut all of that away. After another thirty minutes or so, the driver was freed from the vehicle and transported to the hospital. He had a crushed pelvis, broken femur, broken ribs, and wounds to his head. He lived but will forever walk with a limp.

Foot Pursuit with a Rookie

In 1995, while working downtown I was paired with a new partner. Troy Bookout had just completed the academy and was assigned to my shift. We rode two-man and were working the night shift from 1800 to 0200. One night at about 2300 hours, his first or second shift, we were driving north on Broad Street approaching St. Louis Street when we saw a Black male pushing a shopping cart with a window air conditioner unit in it. The suspect was a well-known thief, so I made the block to come back to him.

As I turned the corner and began approaching the suspect, he walked away from the shopping cart, acting nonchalantly, slowly walking to the gas station. I told Troy that he was going to run when we pulled alongside of him and to wait before exiting the car. Just as I predicted, when the patrol car came alongside, he bolted. Before I could say anything, Troy bolted from the car. At the exact moment he was exiting, I accelerated the car, giving chase without expending needless effort.

I heard Troy yelling to stop the car and as I looked to my right, I saw him hanging on by the top of the door. His feet dragged behind him as I sped alongside the running suspect. I slammed on the brakes, jumped from the car, and chased the suspect down. As I was placing handcuffs on him, I heard someone running up to us and I looked just in time to see Troy leaping in the air, landing on the suspect, and yelling at me for dragging him.

After securing the suspect, we walked him back to the patrol car, I was laughing the whole way, and Troy was fuming. Once the suspect was secured in the back seat, we assessed the damage to Troy's boots. The leather on the top of the toes was scratched and worn down, ruined. Lesson learned for the rookie: Don't run when you can drive.

Serial Vehicle Burglar

One night in the late 1990s, I was riding two-man with Officer J. S. in the downtown area. I was on the passenger side of the patrol car, searching for anything or anyone out of the ordinary. As we drove north on Washington Avenue, just crossing Dauphin Street, I saw Gregory Reiser walking in the shadows. He was carrying a Craftsman toolbox. Knowing Gregory was a serial vehicle burglar and all-around thief, we stopped to investigate. As I approached him on foot, he threw the toolbox and began running north.

I chased him on foot to the north, turning on different streets but making our way towards the Orange Grove Housing Projects. Officer J. S. collected the toolbox and scattered tools then drove towards where we were running in an attempt to get in front of us to head Gregory off. I called out my location as we ran, hoping additional officers were in the area and could quickly respond to assist.

We crossed Congress Street and made out way to N. Broad Street. I began closing on Gregory as we ran east on Broad Street towards where it turns into Beauregard Street. As we approached the intersection of N. Lawrence Street, I pulled my newly issued expandable baton from my gun belt. Gaining on him, I reached out to strike him in the shoulder. Missing, I came down directly on the back of his head. He continued running and almost instantly, Officer J. S. was in front of us spraying his Cap Stun pepper spray. Gregory ran through the orange, toxic cloud, followed closely by me, both of us breathing the pepper into our lungs.

As we turned north on N. Lawrence Street, I was able to take him to the ground. Officer J. S. immediately attempted to place handcuffs on him, but Gregory continued to fight. Suddenly, Officer J. G. arrived on scene and began assisting. Gregory was flailing and kicking as he resisted our attempts to handcuff him, so I struck him in the thigh with my baton. As soon as the baton made impact, a loud bang sounded. It sounded like a gunshot and caused everyone to pause for a split second which allowed us to place the handcuffs on Gregory.

At the exact moment the cuffs were applied, Officer J. G. was hauling ass to his patrol car, fleeing the scene of the "shooting." Officer J. S. and I walked Gregory back to our patrol car that was parked around the corner. When we got to the patrol car, we patted him down and discovered the cause of the fired round. When I struck his thigh, I hit a disposable lighter and it exploded.

Gregory refused to tell us where he had stolen the tools, so we drove back to the area where we first observed him. Backtracking from there, we were able to find a car that had been broken into. Running the tag of the car, we were able to identify the owner. She was the niece of one of our Police Majors, and he was contacted. He was able to make contact with his niece who was at an event at the Civic Center. She came to her car and was able to identify the stolen goods.

The report was written, and we took Gregory to Metro Jail. It had been about an hour-and-a-half since we first engaged with him, and he had made no complaints of injury or pain during the course of the call. As we took him from the backseat of the patrol car while in the sally port of the jail, we saw for the first time the cartoon knot on the back of his head. The knot was huge! It looked like a softball under the skin. The intake deputy called for the jail nurse who came down to take a look. She studied the knot for a few moments and stated, "This is old. We can take him."

As we drove from the jail, I remember thinking it was an old injury, about an hour-and-a-half old. As I gathered my equipment from the trunk of the patrol car and attempted to close my expandable baton, I realized it was bent. That was the first use of the baton, and I realized it was a cheap piece of garbage compared to our old batons.

Gregory was sentenced to fifteen years. His previous record and his probation status helped seal the harsh sentence for a property crime. Several years later, one of our co-workers was in Birmingham for a class, and he ran into Gregory on the street. He asked him why he hadn't come back to Mobile after he was released from prison, and Gregory told him he didn't want to get hit in the head again.

Officer J. G. is a sergeant now, and I still give him a hard time for hauling ass when he heard the "gunshot.". He says he only left because the suspect was in handcuffs, and we had it under control, and he was needed on other calls.

Drunk at Government and Bayou

It never ceases to amaze me that people will get so intoxicated while downtown that they lose all ability to function. Finding people passed out in parking lots, inside bars, the parks, and other places became so common on the weekends you didn't have to drive far to find one.

One night I was riding two-man with another officer when we came upon a male who was passed out drunk on the sidewalk at Government Street and Bayou Street. It was about 2300 hours, and this chap had apparently had enough to drink. He was sprawled out, face down on the sidewalk, with his pants pulled down to his ankles. We made sure he wasn't dead or injured and was just drunk. As we suspected, he was lit, oblivious to everything around him.

As he started to focus and become aware of our presence, I acted as if I had just been chasing someone on foot. I asked him, acting out of breath and concerned, if he knew the guy that was with him. He asked what guy to which I replied the guy who was having sex with you on the pavement. This got the drunk's attention. He looked wide-eyed around and noticed his pants were around his ankles. As he struggled to pull his pants up, I again asked if he knew who the guy he was having sex with was. He stated he wasn't with anyone and refused our offer for a report. He stated he just wanted to go back to his hotel room at the Budget Inn. We took him to the parking lot of the Budget Inn, and let him go to his room to sleep it off.

We were having a little laugh at his expense, until a few hours later we heard the dispatcher dispatch a call of a suspected sexual assault at the Budget Inn to another officer. We jumped the call and sure enough, it was our drunk trying to report his sexual assault. It seems that as he began sobering up, he felt funny, and he had a pain in his rectum so obviously he had been assaulted. It took us a few minutes to convince him that he had not been sexually assaulted, only inappropriately made fun of. I suppose he was mad but even more relieved.

"Robbery" on Dauphin Street

One evening I was working downtown, and it was uncommonly slow. I stopped by Gus's restaurant to chat with an off-duty officer who was working an extra job. We were parked in front of the restaurant, enjoying some ice cream, when we observed two Black males running towards us. They appeared to be in their late teens and were about a block-and-a-half away.

One of the males suddenly turned, running south towards Conti Street while the other approached us and in a panicked voice said the other male had just robbed him. We threw our ice cream out the windows and sped off towards Conti. We saw the suspect, now walking behind the McDonalds. As we exited the car, both of us gave commands for him to stop and get on the ground.

The suspect turned towards us but kept walking backwards, away from us and refusing to comply with commands. We rushed him and were able to catch him and take him to the ground. As we were trying to handcuff him, he began screaming and resisting. Several punches were thrown and pain compliance techniques used on his wrists and shoulders. Finally handcuffed, we were beginning to get him to his feet when the victim of the robbery came running up to us.

Our "victim" was yelling that he was just kidding, We had his cousin, and he wasn't robbed. The handcuffed suspect was obviously alarmed and wondering what the hell was going on. His cousin kept apologizing, saying how he was just joking. We took the handcuffs off and told them both to get the hell out of there and warned the "victim" that if his cousin beat his ass, he deserved it. They were last seen hauling ass towards Broad Street.

Tough Guys on Dauphin Street

Years ago, there was a pool hall on Dauphin Street that always stayed busy. It was usually packed on the weekends and occasionally on a Thursday night. On one particular Thursday night, they had a special, "drinkin with Lincoln," where for five dollars you got a cup and all the draft beer you could handle. It was packed with college kids and other amateur drinkers, so it didn't take long for the calls to start coming in.

After running a few calls there to remove the drunks and underaged kids, we received a disorderly complaint involving two males who were fighting by the pool tables. As me and my partner entered the business, we could hear the two yelling at each other and see them squaring off holding pool cues. They acted as if they wanted to fight, but it was all yelling and putting on a show.

It took a minute to get them to settle down and once the cuffs were on them, they began yelling and threatening each other again. They knew they were safe, so they kept on talking. We walked them to the sidewalk, and they continued to run their mouths, so we handcuffed them to each other around a streetlight pole. You should have seen their faces when we told them to work it out, we would be back after we got some coffee.

We walked across the street to a restaurant that was still open and ordered coffee to go. After a few minutes inside the restaurant, chatting and waiting for the coffee (still in eyesight of the two idiots on the pole), we walked out, drinking our coffee. As we strolled up to the two suspects, we saw the crowd gathered, giving them space but laughing and making fun of them. Once we got to the pole, we observed the two males crying and apologizing to each other as if they were now good friends.

Being sure the "fight" was out of them, we uncuffed them and sent them home with a warning that if they were seen again downtown that night, they would be run into jail. They walked off together towards the parking lot.

The Officer Stephen Green Incident
From Lt. Paul Check

On February 3, 2012, Officer Stephen Green was on patrol in the 5th Precinct going as unit 451. A call came out at the Dollar General at Schillinger Road at Zeigler Boulevard. The call was about a subject attempting to start a fire in the store and possibly trying to rob it. There was an off-duty Traffic Officer on the scene who had called this in.

The off-duty Traffic Officer was taking care of some errands before his afternoon of escorting floats for that evening's Mardi Gras parade and was in the Dollar General shopping when he observed a subject with lighter fluid spraying it on the register counter. The officer approached the subject and confronted him. A struggle followed but the officer was able to pin the subject to the ground and call for assistance.

The on-duty Tactical Response sergeant happened to be passing the area on his way to the range to coordinate some training when he heard the call come out. He stopped at and entered the store and moved to where the officer was and used his handcuffs to secure the subject. As the sergeant was escorting the subject out of the store, he was met by Officer Green.

Officer Green and the sergeant escorted the subject to Officer Green's vehicle where they changed out handcuffs, and the sergeant let Officer Green know the subject had not been searched yet. This was the first time the sergeant had seen Officer Green since he had taught him officer survival in the Police Academy, and he did not know this was the last time he would see Officer Green alive.

Officer Green transported the subject to Police Headquarters where he was interviewed by detectives from the Robbery Unit and processed by the Identification Unit. When completed Officer Green was going to transport the subject to Metro Jail.

I am not sure if it was a slow news day or if something else was going on at Headquarters, but the press was at the back of Headquarters when Officer Green was escorting the subject to his vehicle. The subject was asked why he did it but what he said was foreshadowing of what was going to happen.

He stated in so many words that "You will remember me after this day."

Officer Green drove the subject to the Metro Jail, what he did not know is the subject had a hidden handcuff key which he used to undo one of the cuffs and had a concealed blade which he planned on using at the right moment. Officer Green parked at the Metro Jail in the intake area that had a secure metal door at each end, left his side arm in his vehicle as required, and opened the rear door of his vehicle to let the subject out.

As Officer Green was escorting the subject to the door to be let into the intake area, the subject scratched his nose. This is when Officer Green was made aware that the subject was not cuffed. Officer Green went to take possession of the subject's hand when the subject produced the small, edged weapon and struck Officer Green in the neck several times. Officer Green retreated from the subject and was overcome from the loss of blood. The subject took possession of Officer Green's patrol vehicle and rammed it through the front metal door.

The vehicle was spotted getting on I-10 west bound and a vehicle pursuit ensued which led to Dauphin Island Parkway down to the area of Miami Street. The subject fled on foot and a search began. One of the detectives that responded to the pursuit was checking under a residence when the subject who was hiding under it shot at him, grazing him on the arm. At this time a perimeter was set up around the residence.

During this time, the on-duty Tactical Response Unit along with the oncoming team were at the Academy gym working out and changing over uniforms for the evening Mardi Gras parade. One of the officers heard the call of an officer being assaulted at the Metro Jail and ensuing pursuit, and all units geared up and began to head to the Parkway.

As the Tactical Unit began to arrive on the scene, the sergeants began to deploy their officers to relieve the patrol units on perimeter, and with the Tactical Lieutenant on scene, began to formulate a plan to extract the subject from under the residence.

The Unit first tried to deploy CS gas under the residence to force the subject out. However the previous gun fire from the subject and first responding officers had struck water pipes under the house. The flooding under the house caused the rounds penetrating the mud to be ineffective. The Unit next used 12-gauge slug rounds to try to start removing cinder blocks that were blocking the officer's view.

Unknown to the Team, the subject was in a small bricked-in area used to catch ashes from the fireplace above and was protected from view and scoped rifles. The Tactical commander told the sergeant who had responded to the call earlier that day to form a two-man team with a ballistic shield to approach the side of the house to try to observe the subject. The officer and the sergeant took the shield, jumped a chain link fence, turned the shield sideways, and low-crawled towards the side of the house. As they were trying to observe the subject under the residence, they were told that the Mobile County Sheriff's Office was going to send one of their search and apprehension K9s under the residence.

As the K9 was sent under the residence, it contacted the subject in his hidden position. The K9 began to drag the subject into the open when the subject shot a round at the K9. The K9's handler went under the house to retrieve his dog and he shot at the subject. The Tactical sergeant, seeing this could not let the handler be under the house by himself so he threw off his helmet and tactical vest so he could fit under the house and crawled in to assist. The handler was pulling his dog out from under the house, and at this point the subject was trying to retreat into his hiding spot. The sergeant engaged the subject until his progress stopped.

The sergeant called out cease fire and crawled up to make sure the threat was neutralized. He told other operators to come up to the side of the residence, then he grabbed the subject by the wrist and dragged him to the side of the house so other officers could pull him from underneath the house. The scene was secured as a crime scene and held until Homicide Detectives and Crime Scene Unit could conduct their investigation. The Mardi Gras parade went on as planned.

The Curious Career of Officer Joseph Puckett

Joseph Harry Puckett, an electrician by trade and military veteran, was hired by the Mobile Police Department on August 3, 1970. In his short tenure with the Department, he was involved in several strange incidents. He was wounded in service, filed a lawsuit that changed City and Department policies, and several years after his departure from the Department, was involved in a hostage situation that gained national attention.

Puckett's first few years on the department were relatively uneventful. In December 1971, he was commended for rescuing several young teenagers from a situation in the Maysville area by the director of the Southwest Alabama Council on Alcoholism. He was issued reprimands for minor infractions during that time as well.

On November 2, 1972, things took a turn. He was called to meet a man behind the American Oil Station at Bel Air Mall at about 2140 hours. When he arrived, his car was approached by a male who asked if he was Officer Puckett. When Puckett answered that he was, the man stated that he was a City of Mobile employee who drove a trash truck, and he was upset that Puckett had called his supervisor to complain about him speeding in the trash truck. The male became more belligerent, and Puckett exited his car in an attempt to effect an arrest.

The male began assaulting Puckett, knocking him to the ground and punching him in the face. Citizens in the area attempted to intervene and pull the suspect off of Puckett. As Puckett regained his feet, still dazed by the beating, he saw the suspect lunging for him again. Officer Puckett drew his service weapon and fired one shot, striking the suspect in the stomach.

The suspect was arrested and charged with felony battery on an officer. On October 5, 1973, that suspect signed a release and discharge against Officer Puckett, the City of Mobile, and any other party in exchange for the charges being nolle prossed.

Officer Puckett was suspended without pay for two days on July 17 and 18, 1973. This suspension was for negligence when he wrecked a patrol car on Nevius Road. Five days later on the 23rd of July, a sergeant observed him drinking beer in the parking lot at police headquarters about 1100 hours. He was supposed to be on duty at 1400 hours that day at the airport. The shift lieutenant sent the sergeant who observed Puckett drinking and another sergeant to the airport to investigate. Upon their arrival, they stated that Puckett smelled of alcohol, so they drove him to Headquarters where he was told to take a breath test. He refused and was immediately suspended from duty. Ultimately, he was suspended for thirty days, but that was reduced to twenty-eight days due to the previous two day suspension already served.

In 1953, the Mobile City Commission passed an ordinance, based on the authority granted by Act No. 370 passed by the Alabama Legislature that stated the Chief of Police of the City of Mobile shall have the authority to suspend any personnel or employee of the police department of the City of Mobile, without pay or other compensation and without the right of any hearing or appeal, provided however that no such employee may be suspended by him for a period or periods in the aggregate of more than thirty days in any one calendar year.

On September 25, 1973, at 1100 hours, Puckett was patrolling the area around Michigan Avenue and Tennessee Street when he observed two suspects run from the Shoppers Plaza carrying several suits of clothing. The suspects were closely followed by a store employee who was shouting for the suspects to stop.

Puckett gave chase and was hollering for the suspects to stop. As he gained on one suspect, the suspect turned and pulled a knife, lunging towards the officer. Puckett drew and fired, striking the suspect in the leg. Both suspects were captured and charged with Grand Theft.

On January 12, 1974, Puckett responded to a domestic complaint at 1211 Ghent Street. Upon his arrival, and prior to his backing officer's arrival, Puckett heard a distressed female inside. He entered the residence and saw a male suspect holding a shotgun to a female's head. As Puckett tried to talk the male into dropping the weapon, the suspect pointed the shotgun towards him and said he would kill him. Puckett fired three rounds, the suspect fired as well at point blank range, striking Puckett in the right hand, with buckshot, mangling his hand and disarming him. Puckett ran towards a bedroom, and as he was diving out of the bedroom window to escape the assault, the suspect fired again. This time striking the officer in the back, hip, and leg.

Backup arrived and the suspect surrendered. Puckett was rushed to the hospital where he had surgery to repair the damage done to his body. He lost two fingers on his right hand, and his leg and knee were severely injured, nearly causing paralysis in his foot. After months in the hospital, Puckett was released but unable to return to duty. Additional surgeries and physical therapy were required.

The suspect, Clevon Dixon, was found guilty and sentenced to fifteen years in prison. He appealed his conviction, but the conviction was upheld.

During the summer of 1974, Puckett and several other officers filed a federal lawsuit against the City of Mobile for suspending them without hearings or a right to appeal. On August 14, 1974, in the Federal Court, Chief Judge Pittman issued a summary judgement against the City of Mobile. He ruled that the state law and city ordinance used to suspend officers without pay and without due process or any process to appeal was unconstitutional.

The court did not award damages, but all twenty-two officers involved were given their back pay. The pay ranged from $56.32 for one officer to $628.39 for Puckett, who had been suspended for the longest period of time.

On January 1, 1975, Officer Puckett was medically retired from the Mobile Police Department due to his injuries and ongoing treatment. He was granted a sixty percent retirement which was $450 per month. Officer Puckett did not seek the retirement but was unable to perform the duties of an officer.

On June 30, 1980, things took a turn for the worse for Officer Puckett. He woke that day and drove to Dauphin Street and I-65 to the temporary City Hall. The government offices had been moved there after Hurricane Frederic the year before. Puckett entered Mayor Robert Doyle's office to complain about his medical retirement and his benefits.

At that time, Mobile was governed by a three-person commission. The position of Mayor rotated annually between the three elected commissioners. On June 30, 1980, Robert Doyle was the Public Safety Commissioner as well as the Mayor.

As Puckett entered the office, he produced a .357 handgun and demanded everyone leave the office but him and Doyle. After a short period of time, Puckett demanded the news media to come and bear witness to his grievances.

Puckett held Mayor Doyle hostage for over an hour, all the time complaining about his perceived unfair treatment at being medically retired while he "was still laid up in the hospital" and what he considered to be unfair wages in his retirement package.

After he aired his grievances, he surrendered to officers and was arrested for Kidnapping 1st Degree. His bond was set at $100,000. Puckett spent ten-and-a-half months in jail, awaiting trial. At his trial, he was found guilty of unlawful imprisonment and sentenced to time served.

Puckett accomplished nothing in his unlawful act, even complaining later that his actions only benefited Mayor Doyle, who was running for reelection at the time, in being reelected.

Joseph Puckett died of cancer on April 18, 1985.

A Strange Outcome for a Violent Case

On November 24, 1947, at 6:45 pm. officers assigned to Police Headquarters on St. Emanual Street were notified of an incident in progress on Hamilton Street at Madison Street, at the Lee School. Citizens were reporting that a man was assaulting a young female on the doorsteps of the school.

As the officers arrived at the school, the male suspect attempted to flee on foot but was quickly apprehended. It was soon discovered that he had raped the sixteen-year-old girl.

The young teenager stated that she had been walking home from Murphy High School when she came upon this unknown man, and they began walking together. The two decided to take a bus downtown to see a movie, and she called her mother to tell her she would be home around 7 p.m. as she was helping her schoolteacher. They got off the bus near the Greyhound Bus station on Government Street and Joachim Street and walked to Royal Street, then to Dauphin Street. They walked Dauphin to Washington Avenue and went inside a business where she had a soda, and the male had a beer. After leaving, they walked back down Dauphin to Jackson Street and then south until they got to Galvez Park. She would not go into the park, having heard it was not a nice place to be, so they walked to Lee School on Hamilton.

At the school, the male grabbed her and forced himself on her. Her screams were heard by citizens who alerted the police. At the police station, she provided an account of the events and signed a written statement. She was returned home, and the male was arrested for rape.

On December 10, 1947, just sixteen days after the incident, the case was dismissed. The reason for the dismissal: the victim and suspect had gotten married.

Southern Oaks Shooting

On March 25, 1977, at apartment 1 in the Southern Oaks complex located at 833 University Boulevard, Thomas Duncan and some of his friends started the evening off by having hamburgers and some drinks. His roommate left the apartment to take his girlfriend to the movies, and Duncan asked his two female roommates to go to the store to buy some Sprite to mix with the Canadian Mist he had.

When the girls returned to the apartment, Duncan was acting strangely. He began blasting the stereo, acting as if he were high on something. He grabbed another roommate's guitar and started aggressively strumming it, using a key for a guitar pick and causing damage. The girls decided they should leave. As they were preparing to leave for the evening, Duncan went outside and cranked up his roommate's car. He floored the accelerator, racing the engine until it began to smoke and coolant poured from the engine. Walking back inside, Duncan acted as if nothing was wrong.

Around 0050 hours on March, 26, 1977, a neighbor called the police to report a report of a disorderly coming from apartment 1. Officer Homer Floore was dispatched and while en route, he was advised there had been shots fired in the area. Officer Floore arrived on the scene at 0055 hours. He was flagged down by a white male who advised that he was the person who called the police. As Officer Floore was still seated in his patrol car, speaking with the man in the parking lot, a shot rang out. Floore stated that he felt pain in his legs and there was glass and debris covering him. The man he had been speaking to had run for cover.

Officer Floore put his patrol car in drive and drove about one hundred fifty feet to the east in the parking lot, where he exited and took cover behind his patrol car. He notified the operator that he had taken fire and had been wounded.

Officer Floyd Burch was dispatched as the backing for Officer Floore, and as he was turning into Southern Oaks Apartments, he heard Officer Floore's radio traffic about being shot. Officer Burch looked towards apartment 1 and saw a white male standing at the bottom of the stairs holding either a shotgun or a rifle, and he was pointing it towards Officer

Floore. Before he could take evasive action, the male (Thomas Duncan) turned towards him and fired a round into the windshield of Burch's patrol car. The buckshot from the shotgun struck Burch in the right shoulder. Burch attempted to back out of the area, but the car would not move. Duncan fired a couple more rounds into Burch's car, striking Officer Burch with pellets and glass debris. Burch was able to exit the car and crawl to the back of it, taking cover until Sergeant Grissett arrived on scene and had him lay on the ground until they could get an ambulance to him.

As this was unfolding, Officer Benny Twiggs had been called by the apartment answering service to respond to a loud music complaint at apartment 1. Officer Twiggs worked as the security officer for the apartment complex when he was not on duty with the Police Department. As he was approaching apartment 1 to tell them to turn the music down, he heard several gunshots ring out. As he got closer, he was informed by an unknown resident what was taking place. He made his way to the south and met up with Sergeant Wayne Ivey, and they worked their way towards the other officers. After a brief period, Officer Twiggs left and went to the apartment complex office where he was able to access the renter files on the person who resided in apartment 1. He obtained a layout of the apartment as well as the telephone number for the occupant.

Sergeant Raymond Grissett, Sergeant Pete Holifield, and Sergeant Frank Woodward arrived on the scene at the same time. As they exited their cars, Duncan fired four or five rounds at them, striking two patrol cars. The officers returned fire with their revolvers, but that did not stop Duncan from continuing to fire on them. Sergeant Holifield moved to the east side of the parking lot to deploy arriving officers in critical positions around apartment 1.

Officer Wilbur Williams heard the call on the radio, and he responded from Azalea Road. When he drove into the parking lot, he pulled just past Officer Burch's car and saw a white male step to the window of the apartment, raise a shotgun and point it at him. As Officer Williams was exiting his car, Duncan fired the shotgun, striking Williams windshield, covering Williams with the shattered glass. Officer Williams returned fire with his revolver. Williams moved to cover on the south side of the apartment where he was later joined by Sergeant Holifield. During the course of the event, Duncan fired several rounds at Williams and Holifield, striking the car they were taking cover behind.

Lieutenant Charles Sullivan arrived on the scene and proceeded on foot to the position held by Sergeant Grissett and Officer Burch. Duncan fired four or five rounds at Lieutenant Sullivan as he made his way to the position.

Jim's Ambulance Service was dispatched to pick up Officer Burch. Michael White and Ronald Newman responded to the scene. They parked on University and approached on foot with a canvass stretcher. As they approached Officer Burch and began treating him, they observed pellet wounds to Burch's face and blood smeared across his forehead. As they were assessing Officer Burch, Duncan fired rounds towards the patrol car they were taking cover behind. The shotgun pellets struck the rear of the patrol car, shattering the taillights, also striking the pavement, sending debris into the medics. They were not seriously injured.

Chief Donald Riddle, Major Winston Orr, and Lieutenant Walter Milne arrived on the scene at the command post. SWAT was called out at 0210 hours. The SWAT team, comprised of Sergeant Jessie Robertson, Officer Phillip Tipp, Officer Rassie Smith, Officer Nolan Ramsey, and Officer Steve Scarcliff, responded to the precinct at 1251 Virginia Street and gathered their equipment and prepared for the deployment. They loaded into the paddy wagon. Sergeant Jessie Robertson was in charge of the responding SWAT team. As the SWAT team was making its way to the scene, officers already deployed there evacuated persons from nearby apartments and held the perimeter. All the while, they were being shot at by Duncan.

All on-duty officers responded to the scene and calls for service in the city were handled by the Mobile County Sheriff's Department. Sheriff Tom Purvis and a couple deputies responded to the scene as well.

At about 0430, Duncan's father and minister arrived on the scene. They attempted to talk to him through a bullhorn. After several failed attempts to get Duncan to talk, it was determined that tear gas would be deployed.

SWAT took up positions around the apartment and were assisted by Officers Bobby Jackson, Lester Hargrove, Benny Twiggs, Vernon Straum, Wayne Farmer, and Sergeant Presnall.

Four rounds of tear gas were shot into the lower windows and the second story windows. A few minutes later, the glass on the first floor was breached and a handheld tear gas grenade was thrown in. After a few minutes, Duncan came to the door, raised his hands and surrendered, cursing and threatening the whole time. Officers Rassie Smith, Phillip Tipp, James Mayo, Robert Duff, Robert Osborn, and Sergeant Robinson took him into custody. Duncan was wearing an ammo belt on his waist when captured. He was handcuffed and transported to headquarters.

Both injured officers were transported to University Medical Center where they were treated by Doctor Snodgrass. Officer Floore was treated for gunshot wounds to both legs, and Officer Burch was treated for gunshot wounds to the head, shoulder, and side. Both were released that night.

Identification officers Lieutenant Long and Officer Ronnie Myers responded to the scene. Two 12 gauge shotguns, a lever action .30-30, and a .243 Winchester rifle with a scope were recovered from inside the apartment along with an assortment of ammunition, drug paraphernalia, marijuana seeds, and alcohol.

The criminal investigation was conducted by Sergeants Ashbel White, O.C. Lockett, and Bessie Ibsen. Sergeant Joe Connick submitted an inventory of the damaged patrol cars. The damage was extensive to some of the cars rendering them undrivable. His report listed the vehicle by asset number and indicated the total number of bullet holes and locations of the strikes for each vehicle.

The following is his report:

Asset 2961
4-in windshield
1-on windshield frame
2-driver's door
4-grill, radiator, air conditioner
11 total

Asset 2938
10-right rear
1-right rear tire

1-right front, through fender, dash, seat
2-hood, fan, radiator, fanbelt, battery case and hose
6-windshield and frame
1-grill
1-bumper
1-headlight, right side
2-left door
1-left headlight
26 total

Asset 2956
7-windshield and frame
1-right front under headlight
2-grill and condenser
1-right front tire
1-rear windshield
1-rear window-broke out
5-entrance to left front door
2-from inside left door
1-blue light-right side
21 total

Asset 2939
1-through left front door, hit lower steering wheel
1 total

Asset 2937
1-dent in right quarter panel

Asset 2974, car 2K6
3-windshield
2-grill through air conditioner condenser
1-left rear rain gutter
6 total

There was an additional civilian vehicle struck by gunfire that was parked across University Boulevard from the apartment. That vehicle, a 1976 Pontiac, was struck in the door with the bullet travelling through the floor. A bullet was recovered and identified as a .30-30 round. Identification Officer R. Myers measured the distance from the apartment to the parked vehicle and determined it was four hundred seventy-three feet.

Thomas Duncan was charged with two counts of assault with intent to murder and six counts of assaulting a police officer with a deadly weapon. The recommended bond of $80,000 was reduced to $60,000. If bond was posted, Duncan would be required to live with his parents. On March 29, 1977, Duncan was released on bond. On September 19, 1977, Duncan pleaded guilty to eight counts of assaulting an officer with a deadly weapon. He was released from prison in 1985.

Morale Building and Camaraderie

Officer Gerry Smith began creating drawings which told the stories of current events on the Department. He started his doodles in the late 1970s and continued through the 1990s. Hundreds of these comedic insights were created over the years. No officer, regardless of rank, no public official, or circumstance was off limits. His lighthearted sketches made fun of officers and situations that brought levity to the men and women of the Department, both sworn and civilian. Sergeant Smith retired from the Mobile Police Department on January 1, 2003. Here are a few of his sketches.

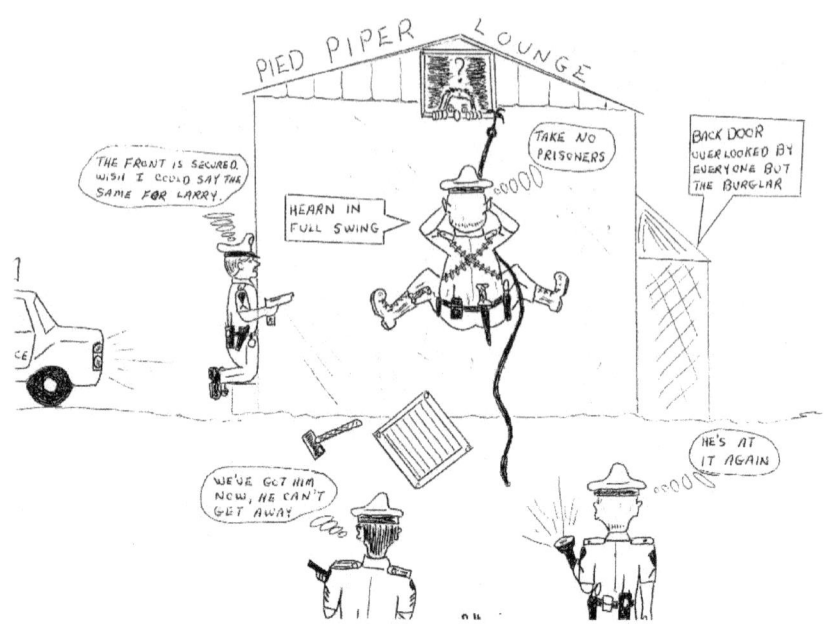

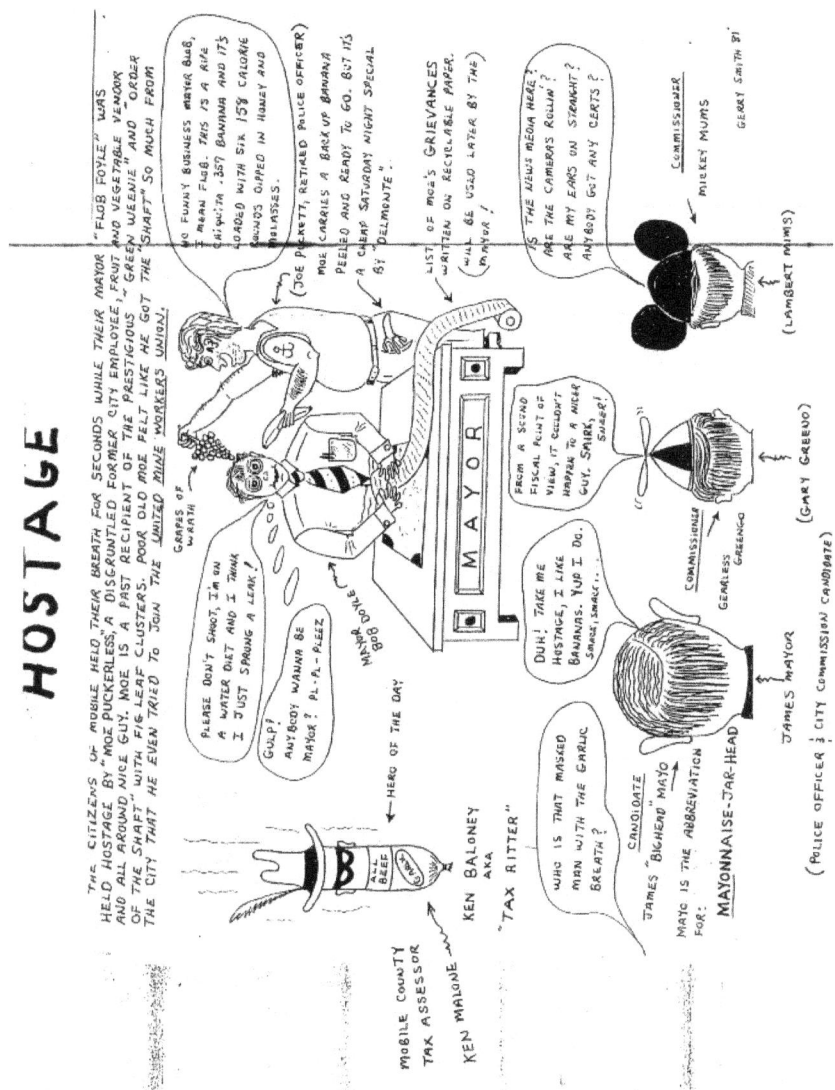

279

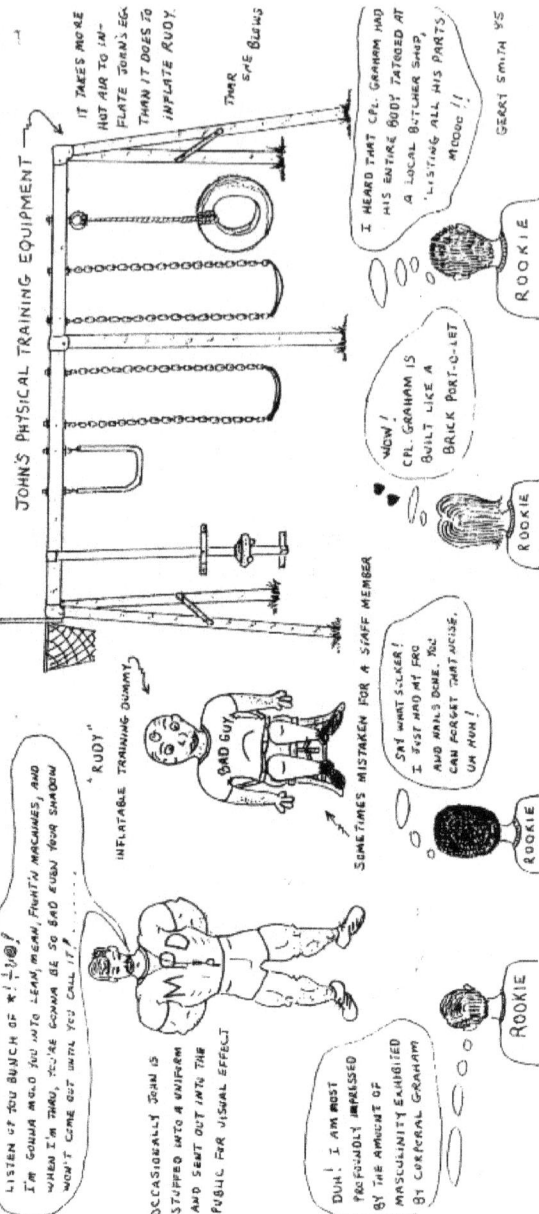

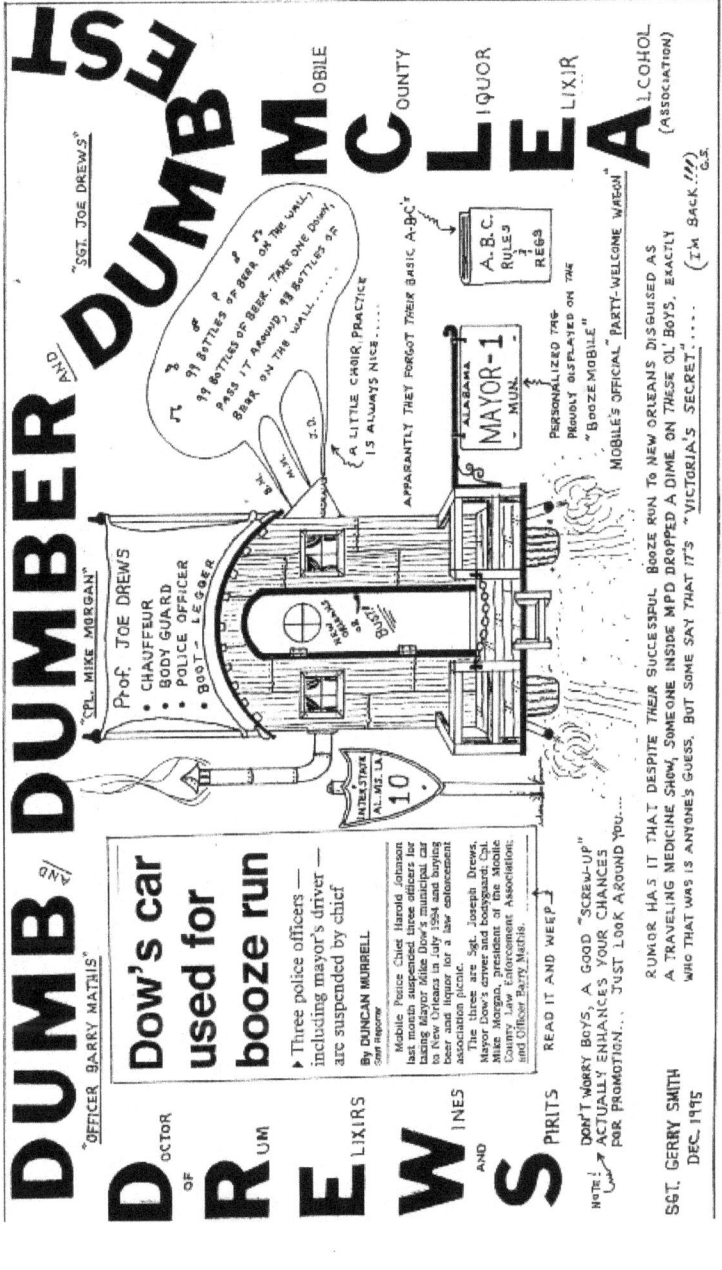

Fallen Officers

These final pages are dedicated to the officers who have made the ultimate sacrifice for their community. Their sacrifice should not be forgotten, no matter how long ago they laid their life down for the security and safety of the citizens of Mobile.

Officer Jerry Lynch

On May 28, 1872, the newspaper reported than on the previous night, May 27, 1872, at approximately 10 o'clock pm, Officer Jerry Lynch had suffered a severe gash wound to the left side of his chest and was rushed to the Guard House for treatment.

Further facts reveal that Officers Lynch and Finnegan were attempting to arrest a Black male subject for Disorderly Conduct on Royal Street between Madison Street and Canal Street. A group of four to five other Black males attacked Officers Lynch and Finnegan, and during this assault, Officer Lynch suffered a stab wound to the left chest.

Officer Lynch died on the evening of Monday, June 3, 1872, and his funeral was held on Tuesday, June 4, 1872, at 3 o'clock pm from St. Vincent's Church. The "Daily Register" reported on June 5, 1872:

> Funeral of Officer Lynch. - the funeral of Officer Jerry Lynch, who died from the effect of a wound inflicted by a group of negro ruffians while in the discharge of his duty, took place yesterday afternoon from St. Vincent's Church, and was very largely attended. The

police force, ninety-one strong, turned out in their new uniforms, and the St. Patrick's Benevolent Association, of which the deceased was an honorable member, were present in full force. the funeral cortege, which was headed by the brass band of Phoenix Fire Co. No. 6, presented a solemn and imposing appearance. Officer Lynch was a zealous, faithful and efficient officer, and dying as he did in the execution of his duty, it has been suggested that the public should make some provision for the support of his helpless family, consisting of a wife and three or four children. We know that our people are heavily taxed for charitable and other objects, but in this case, a most deserving one, we trust that something will be done.

(There is no known photograph of Officer Lynch.)

JEREMIAH LYNCH
Police Officer
Mobile (AL) Police Department
End of Watch: June 3, 1872

Edward McGrath Morris

Detective Edward Morris was shot and wounded on March 31, 1901, at the Mobile, Jackson and Kansas City railyard located at Tennessee and Conception Street. Detective Morris, Patrolman John Bressingham, and Patrolman Edward McGrath were attempting to arrest two escaped convicts when the incident occurred. Detective Morris and Patrolman Bressingham were both shot by one of the escapees. The suspect who fired on the officers was killed by the officers. The second suspect was captured a few miles from the incident location later that afternoon.

Detective Morris died of his wounds at 8:30 pm on April 1, 1901. Morris was a twenty-five-year veteran with the Mobile Police Department.

Charles Haggerty

On December 30, 1903, at around 3 am, Officer Charles Haggerty was shot and killed by an unknown person on Royal Street near Conti Street, just two blocks from police headquarters. His killer was never identified according to available records.

Irish born Officer Haggerty was forty-eight years old and had served four years with the Mobile Police Department.

James J. Shaw

Police Officer James J. Shaw, age twenty-eight, was stabbed and killed on December 21, 1924, as he and several other officers investigated a burglary at a grocery store at Clay Street and Glennon Avenue. During the assault, Officer Shaw was able to draw his weapon and fire at the suspect several times. The suspect was found deceased from those gunshots at his home a few days later.

Officer Shaw had only served eighteen months with the Mobile Police Department.

Chris M. Dean

Police Officer Chris M. Dean was shot and killed early in the morning on January 22, 1926, as he was checking four suspicious men at Davis Avenue and Maple Street. Officer Dean suffered multiple gunshot wounds and was never able to draw his weapon. The assailant was captured shortly after. He was tried for the murder of Officer Dean and convicted. He was executed by hanging on June 25, 1926, at the Mobile County Jail. This is the last known execution to take place in Mobile.

W.F. "Happy" Murphy

Motorcycle Traffic Officer W.F. ("Happy") Murphy was shot and killed on October 18, 1929, at approximately 2 am as he was checking a speeding automobile on Broad Street near Conti Street in downtown Mobile.

The suspect's vehicle was later found abandoned near Picayune, Mississippi. The automobile had been stolen in Jackson, Mississippi, on October 17, 1929. Three weeks later, a tip led to the arrest of a twenty-three-year-old gunman. The suspect was convicted and sentenced to death but was granted another trial. Again, he was convicted and sentenced to death. He was granted a third trial, and the sentence was changed to life on April 6, 1931. He was paroled on February 8, 1946. Murphy left behind a wife and three daughters.

Edward P. DeFord

    Police Officer Edward P. DeFord was shot and wounded on October 30, 1935, as he and his partner, Officer Ed Qualls, were escorting non-union workers across the I.L.A. picket lines near the Port of Mobile at Conception Street and Sumpter Street. Both officers returned fire, killing the suspect. Officer Deford died on October 31, 1935, at 2:35 p.m.

    The I.L.A. strike began across the Gulf Coast ports to try and force shippers to recognize them and give the union contracts. At the time, the I.L.A. was not recognized. There had already been two killings in Lake Charles, Louisiana, related to the strikes. On Wednesday, October 30, 1935, Officer DeFord and his scout car partner, Ed Qualls, were dispatched to Joachim and Marion Streets where a Black male stated he was prevented by the strikers from getting to his job.

The officers drove the man to the job site at Conception Street and Sumpter Street when the male pointed out the five Black males who blocked his entry. The suspects attempted to walk away and when ordered to stop, one of the men, Ernest Dukes, turned and fired eleven rounds from a German Luger, striking Officer DeFord three times. He was struck in the right shoulder, leg, and foot. The officers returned fire, striking and killing Dukes. Another male with Dukes fired one or two shots from a .32 semi-automatic that jammed. The male threw the gun down and ran away. About twenty shots were fired during the incident. The bullet that struck Officer DeFord's shoulder traveled towards his spine and lodged in his left abdomen. He was paralyzed from the chest down. He succumbed to his injury the following day.

Officer Deford was a veteran of eight years with the Mobile Police Department.

Cody Bettis

On August 3, 1938, at 7 am, Motorcycle Traffic Officer Cody Bettis was escorting a military convoy on St. Louis Street. He was struck and killed by an automobile, which broke through the convoy at St. Louis and Jefferson Street. The driver was charged with manslaughter.

Ollie Mason

Police Officer Ollie Mason was shot and killed on June 15, 1943, at 3:45 pm as he and his partner answered a domestic complaint on South Hamilton Street with another officer. As they arrived on scene, the suspect opened fire, striking all three officers. Officer Mason was struck in the leg, the bullet severing the femoral artery. He died on the scene.

Pierce Lee "Rudy" Reeves

Motorcycle Traffic Officer Pierce Lee ("Rudy") Reeves, thirty-two, was killed instantly on September 24, 1944, when the motorcycle he was operating struck an open manhole on Virginia Street at Tuttle Avenue.

Officer Reeves served four years with the Mobile Police Department.

Earl Royce Williams

Traffic Officer Earl Royce Williams was struck and later died of injuries suffered in a hit and run collision, which occurred on June 21, 1968, on the Cochrane Causeway.

Officer Williams was directing traffic around another wreck when he was struck and injured. Officer Williams died on June 24, 1968. Officer Williams was thirty-two years old and served four years with the Mobile Police Department.

Joseph P. Brunson

Motorcycle Traffic Officer Joseph P. Brunson was killed when the motorcycle he was operating left the road on Howell's Ferry Road and struck a mailbox post on May 15, 1975.

Officer Brunson served two years with the Mobile Police Department and seven years with the Prichard Police Department.

Henry Johnny Booth

Police Officer Henry Johnny Booth was shot and killed on August 14, 1979, while attempting to arrest a wanted subject on an outstanding warrant.

Officer Booth was pronounced dead shortly after the 7:55 pm incident. Officer Booth served eight years with the Mobile Police Department.

Julius Schulte

Juvenile Detective Julius Schulte was shot and killed as he answered a domestic complaint involving a missing child on April 18, 1985.

Detective Schulte was a twenty-two-year veteran with the Mobile Police Department.

Douglas E. Kountz

Police Officer Douglas E. Kountz was killed on May 2, 1992, in a one-car accident while responding to a call for assistance from a fellow officer.

Officer Kountz had only served eleven months with the Mobile Police Department.

Owen P. McClinton

Motorcycle Traffic Corporal Owen P. McClinton was killed on December 13, 1996. Corporal McClinton was en route to a traffic assignment when his motorcycle was struck by a vehicle. The driver of that vehicle left the scene of the accident.

Corporal McClinton was a twelve-year veteran of the Mobile Police Department. On December 23, 1996, the vehicle involved was traced, and the owner admitted responsibility. The owner was on parole when he fled the scene.

Rufus Earle Brown

During Mardi Gras in 1993, Corporal Brown responded to a call of a drunk male subject causing a disturbance. When Corporal Brown arrived on the scene, the subject fought him and beat his head against a cement curb. The injuries suffered by Corporal Brown caused him to experience seizures that led to his early retirement.

On March 23, 1997, Corporal Brown suffered a grand mal seizure and died as result. Corporal Brown was fifty-three-years old at time of the incident and had served twenty-six years with the Mobile Police Department before retiring.

Matthew Thompson

Police Corporal Matthew Thompson was killed on February 11, 2004, while assisting officers with a traffic accident on Springhill Avenue. A vehicle traveling westbound on Springhill Avenue struck Corporal Thompson while he was standing near a disabled vehicle that was to be towed. Corporal Thompson later died at the hospital. No criminal charges were brought against the driver.

Corporal Thompson was an eighteen-year veteran of the Mobile Police Department.

Brandon Sigler

Officer Brandon Sigler was killed June 2, 2009, while serving as a courtesy officer at a West Mobile apartment complex where he resided. He was responding to an altercation in the parking lot when he was shot and killed by an eighteen-year-old man. Officer Sigler succumbed to his injuries, leaving behind a devoted family and fiancé.

Officer Sigler served nearly two years with the Mobile Police Department and was assigned to the First Precinct.

Steven Green

Officer Steven Green was fatally wounded on February 3, 2012, after a twenty-four-year-old robbery suspect stabbed him at the Mobile County Metro Jail. His wife was left widowed and three children fatherless.

Officer Green had served for almost two years and was assigned to the Fifth Precinct.

Justin Billa

Officer Justin Billa was shot and killed during a homicide investigation at the 2000 block of Avondale Court on February 20, 2018, at approximately 9:50 pm. The suspect fired multiple shots at officers on the scene, and one round struck Officer Billa. Officer Billa was transported to the hospital where he later died. SWAT officers found his killer deceased inside the residence from a self-inflicted gunshot wound.

Officer Billa served on the force for two years. He was twenty-seven years old.

Sean Tuder

Officer Sean Tuder was shot and killed on Sunday, January 20, 2019. Officer Tuder was scheduled to be off duty that day, but when he received information from an informant about the whereabouts of a wanted suspect, he went to the location, Peach Place Inn. Backup officers were dispatched. When Officer Tuder pulled into the parking lot, the suspect approached his car. During a scuffle before backup arrived, the suspect shot Officer Tuder. Officer Tuder was transported to the hospital where he died as a result of his injuries. His killer was tried, convicted, and sentenced to death.

Officer Tuder was thirty years old. He had joined the Mobile Police Department in March 2016.

Bibliography and Recommended Reading

1. Mobile Police Department documents, reports and photographs

2. Mobile County Public Library, archives

3. Press Register news articles

4. City of Mobile Archives, census data, reports

5. 1927 City of Mobile directory

6. Catholic Cemeteries Historical Documents, Tilmon Brown, Director

7. University of Alabama, Special Collections Library, Mobile Police Department Records, 1865-1869, MSS-1005

8. Historic Mobile Preservation Society's Minnie Mitchell Archives on the Oakleigh Complex

9. Civil War Archives, Rebel Archives, Record Division, War Department

10. *The National Police Journal,* April 1918, G.J. Flournoy, page 12.

11. *Down the Years, Articles on Mobile's History,* Gulf Coast Historical Review

12. *Remember Mobile,* Caldwell Delaney, 1948 1969 published by the Haunted Book Shop, page 138

13. *Craighead's Mobile*, by Caldwell Delaney, 1968 published by the Haunted Book Shop

14. *Mobile of the Five Flags*, Peter J. Hamilton, 1913, the Gill Publishing Company

15. *Colonial Mobile*, Peter J. Hamilton, 1910, University of Alabama Press

16. *Brief Historical Sketches of Military Organizations Raised in Alabama During the Civil War*, by Willis Brewer and John C. Rigdon

About the Author

Billie Rowland was born and raised in southwest Missouri, where he developed a love for history and public service. After serving in the Coast Guard, he started his law enforcement career with the Jasper County Missouri Sheriff's Department in 1989. He joined the Mobile Police Department in April 1992 and has been an officer there since. Billie has a bachelor's degree in criminal justice administration. During his tenure with the Mobile Police Department, he has been promoted through the ranks to captain and has worked downtown, supervised patrol squads in Precinct 1, Precinct 4, served as an Executive Officer in Precinct 3, and he has been the Commander of Central Events and Mounted Unit, Commander of the Support Services Section and Commander of Precinct 4.

His love for Mobile and the Mobile Police Department grew as he worked the Downtown beat. Working in the historic district, he met merchants and residents who had lived and worked there for decades, and listening to their stories of the city fueled his desire to know its history.

The Mobile Police Museum was located in the Central Events Precinct while he was assigned there as an officer and then later as the Precinct Commander, giving him access to some of the department history. When the precinct was moved and the museum closed, he along with Assistant Chief Hodge inventoried the museum contents and then boxed and placed them into storage. His years of research has led to an extensive library and collection of artifacts and finally this book.

Billie and his wife Laury have a daughter, Corey, and a granddaughter, Jordyn. He and Laury have a small ranch and enjoy taking care of their horses, miniature donkeys, alpacas, miniature bull, chickens, turkeys, ducks, rabbit, cats, dogs and water dragon.